GET REAL

A PRACTICAL GUIDE ON HOW TO LIVE IT UP.

LIEN DE PAU

FOR THOSE WHO WANT
TO UNLEASH THEIR
PURPOSE, DO WHAT THEY
LOVE AND LIVE FREELY.

 WWW.FACEBOOK.COM/GETREALBYLIEN

 WWW.GETREALBYLIEN.COM

 HELLO@GETREALBYLIEN.COM

TABLE OF CONTENT

LOOKING FOR MORE INSPIRATION?

When people inspire you for who they are or for what they do, then you should not hide your admiration. That is why I am referring in this book to a couple of people who have inspired me to live a rich life and make my dreams come true. It is because of them I am living it up.

So thank you to each and every one of you for sharing your wisdom and experiences via your blogs, your books and your podcasts.

Tim Ferriss
'The 4-Hour Work Week'
ISBN 9780091929114

Elle Luna
'The Crossroads of Should and Must'
ISBN 9780761184881

Tara Mohr
'Playing Big'
ISBN 9780099591528

Stephen Covey
'The 7 Habits of Highly Effective People'
ISBN 9781451639612

Andre Agassi
'Open'
ISBN 9780307388407

Kelly McGonigal
http://kellymcgonigal.com

Steve Pavlina
https://www.stevepavlina.com

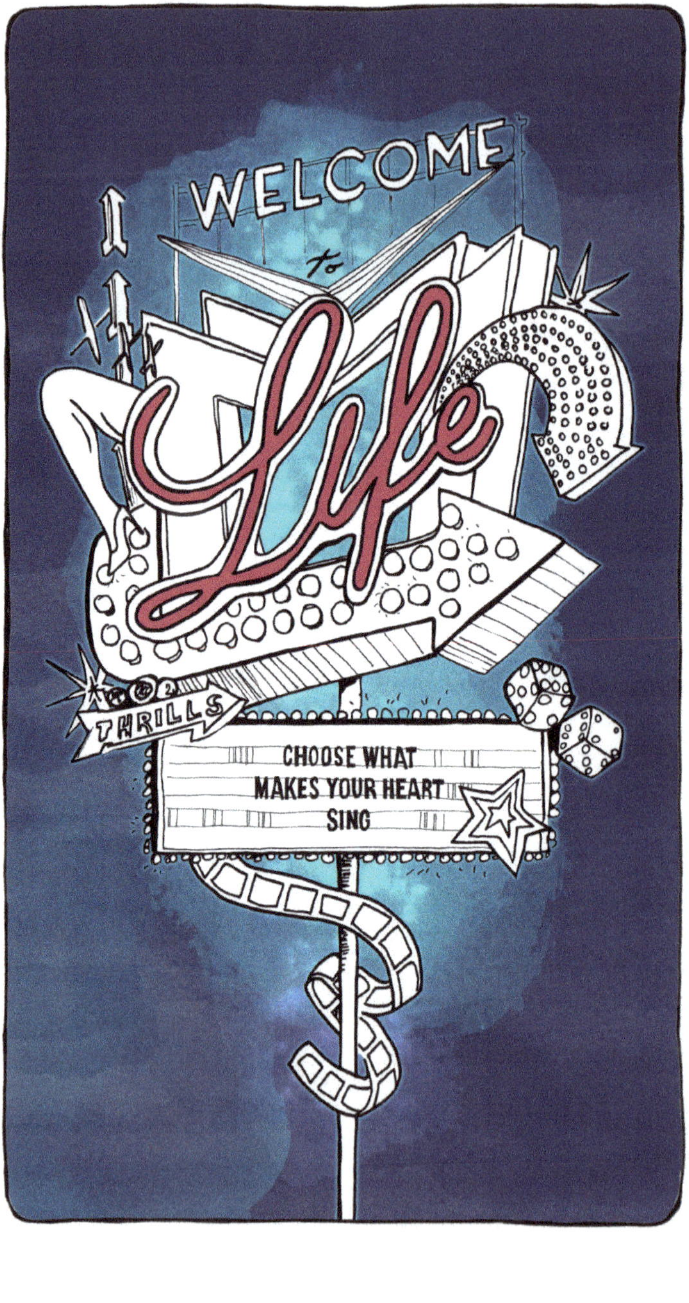
WELCOME
to
Life
THRILLS
CHOOSE WHAT
MAKES YOUR HEART
SING

My Story and Why This Book is Something For You.

CAUTION! - IF YOU WANT TO DIE FULL OF REGRETS, STOP READING NOW.

"HOW THE HELL do you manage to go surfing [every day] while I have to respond at 1:40am because I only have the time and headspace now to actually write to you?!"

March 2016. Sender of this message: Annelies, my publisher. Her message to me will become the starting point of the book you are holding in your hands right now. In Get Real you will discover how I succeeded to transform myself from slave to surfer. How 4 years ago I re-organised my hectic life so I could drive to the Longneck Tribe in Vietnam, dive with sharks in the Galapagos and hike up a 4700 metre peak in the Peruvian mountains. Even though my adventures throughout 40 countries are the backbone of this book, this is not a travel diary full of practical travel hacks. But if you are looking for the essential keys to die without any regrets, this is the book you have been looking for.

DOING WHAT IS EXPECTED OF YOU IS THE FASTEST ROAD TO DESTINATION BOREDOM.

Most people — and that is likely including you, as you are reading this book — realise at a certain moment in their life that the path which was predefined for them, is not the one that makes them crazy happy. Unfortunately, only a handful of people actually succeed in creating and walking a path of their own. The question "What do I really want to do with my life" is easy to ask, but so damn hard to answer.

Until 2011 I did what was expected from me. My life was fine. There was nothing really wrong with it. But it didn't make my heart beat faster. I was playing safe. This all felt like an itchy spot that was just out of reach: slightly annoying, but not a reason to throw yourself off a bridge. Until, out of the blue, my world fell apart and I had a good reason to throw myself off that bridge. While I was trying to convince myself not to, it very quickly became clear that I had nothing to hold onto: no backbone, no inner compass and no foundation. I was teetering on the edge, my body dangerously tilting towards the ravine and there was no bungee rope in reach. There, on the edge, I received the bill for doing exactly what was expected of me, without me ever considering if I was actually happy.

DON'T MAKE IT WORSE THAN IT ALREADY IS. STOP RUNNING AROUND LIKE A HEADLESS CHICKEN. NOW.

In the first chapter of this book you'll read all about my most clumsy attempts to find out what I wanted to do with my life. Because despite all the self-help books I collected over the years, finding my own path was not exactly a walk in the park. Instead, my search for a more fulfilling life went across a white sandy beach in Kenya and the cool tiles of a Hindu temple in Malaysia. I believe that my path will inspire you to discover what you truly want out of life. But don't worry, you don't have to walk in my international footsteps (unless you want to) in order to find out what you truly want. Feel free to simply settle comfortably in the sofa with this book and discover from there how you can stop running around like a headless chicken.

You know... I've never met someone who said: "It has always been my dream to get up at 7am five days a week, drive to work and (pretend to) be very busy and important, to be stuck in a traffic jam around 6pm on my way home, just to throw myself onto the sofa and dream about the next weekend to come, which will be packed with forced "relaxation". Only to have it all start again the next "Monday". So why do we collectively spend our days this way and call it life?

> "SO
> WHY DO WE
> COLLECTIVELY
> SPEND OUR DAYS
> THIS WAY AND
> CALL IT LIFE?"

Maybe all you ever really want in life is to be an isolated writer hidden somewhere deep in the mountains, sweating over this one masterpiece for years. Or perhaps you want to spend your life strolling to your hammock every day and contemplate the tides of the ocean while sipping an exotic cocktail. Maybe you want to put all your energy, time and money in empowering single mums. Or you might want to get up every day without an alarm clock and do what you would love to do most that day. Just like me.

In the first two chapters of Get Real, I will tell you which approach, of the dozens I tested, finally helped me discover how I really want to live my life. And that seemed to be completely different from what most of us consider 'normal'.

CHOOSE YOUR OWN PATH AND EXPECT A LOT OF CRITICISM. MAINLY FROM YOURSELF.

"That's impossible!"

Once you discover that your true path is not that well-paved and well-travelled road, you immediately realise how strong the forces are that want to keep you on the path which was destined for you. Expect a lot of criticism; mainly from yourself. Strong beliefs like 'everybody has to work and that's just the way it is', 'who am I to do such a thing', 'if you want to buy nice things, you just have to work really hard' or 'sometimes you have to do things you hate, it's part of life' will be on endless repeat in your mind. These are strong beliefs taught to all of us by our family and friends, the culture in which we grow up and the society we live in:

"Just do like everyone else, that's crazy enough already". These beliefs are limiting you every single day in changing your life for the better and they ensure that you (and millions of others) stick to conformity, normality and living an average life.

'JUST ACT NORMAL' IS SO INCREDIBLY TEMPTING.

Despite the fact that Western society allows us more and more freedom, you are still expected to explain to other people as to why you are not doing what everyone else is doing. As a woman, you still have to justify why you don't want children. As a man, you need to justify why you are choosing to be a stay-at-home dad. And if you give up your well-paid, secure job to develop your own business, you'd better have a very good reason for it. Our society wants us to get a steady job in order to pay off the mortgage on that house with the nice garden, to marry our partner and to raise one (or two) children. This is the dream society has for all of us and it'd better be your dream too.

Well, I stopped doing what everyone else is doing and created my own dreams.

"I STOPPED DOING WHAT EVERYONE ELSE IS DOING AND CREATED MY OWN DREAMS"

Not because I felt the urge to rebel, but simply because, in the last couple of years, I became more and more true to myself and my own unique path. When choosing your own path, you have to anticipate the bumpy road ahead, full of obstacles and risks. How I managed these so-called risks is part of the story I want to share with you in this book. I will explain how I overcame the fear that comes with taking these risks and how I managed those moments where I doubted myself so much that all I wanted to do was cry, give up and return to doing what everyone else wanted me to do. I am sharing all this openly and in all honesty with you in chapter four of this book. The fact that my regained life happened to be a fantastic rollercoaster full of adventure, fulfilment and a feeling of happiness that I had never ever experienced before was a great help. In this book I will show you where I found the courage (completely overrated in my case) and the willpower (which actually does not exist) to escape the overwhelming force which pulls us all back to an average life. And if I am able to escape from this force, then why wouldn't you be?

FOLLOW YOUR OWN PATH AND GET AN EXCLUSIVE ENTRY TICKET TO THE MOST AMAZING THEME PARK IN THE WORLD.

Congratulations! And welcome!

From the moment you discover what you really want to do with your life and once you have found the courage to keep on walking your unique path, you will get rewarded with an entry ticket to the playground that is called life. And then the fun really begins! When I got to this point in my life and in my personal development, I felt like Mario who finally reached a higher level in Super Mario Land.

In this next phase of my more fulfilling life, I was able to do some amazing things which I previously never even dared to dream of. I travelled across Asia for 2 years with a backpack of no more than 10 kilos. I learned how to scuba dive and how to drive a motorbike. I also learned how to keep my balance on a surfboard. And thanks to a trip across South-America, I finally got to learn Spanish (something I'd dreamed about for more than 15 years).

But besides all these personal achievements (which were completely focused on 'me, myself and I') I slowly but surely started to create valuable things for other people too - the launch of a network for female entrepreneurs being the most recent one.

> "THE GOOD NEWS IS THAT YOU CAN GET YOUR OWN TICKET TO THIS PLAYGROUND!"

The good news is that you can get your own ticket to this playground!

When you know what you really want in life and when you have found the courage to walk your own unique path, you can leave your own personal footprint. You can mean an awful lot to yourself, your family, your children, the society in which you live and the world. It is only then that you are making use of the real potential you carry inside you. Only then you can exceed yourself in ways you never thought possible.

DOUBTERS AND SCEPTICS, THIS IS FOR YOU...

WHAT YOU SHOULD KNOW BEFORE READING.

You'll definitely recognise this... that question you ALWAYS get when meeting someone new. 'And what do you do?' You are expected to answer by giving your job title. I always found it strange that your very existence is narrowed down to the things you do to make money.

When I meet someone new (and being a fulltime nomad and world citizen, this happens all the time), my answer to the question 'What do you do?' is always the same: 'What I love to'.

Most people react to my answer with an uncomfortable silence. I can see from their facial expression that the neurons inside their brain are going wild. Because doing what you love every single day is 'obviously completely bonkers'. So I end up explaining how I did it. How I managed to build a life in which I only do what I love to do every single day.

As always, a lot of questions are fired at me. Sometimes people are looking for confirmation as to why they would definitely not be able to do what they love every single day. And other times people want to know if they could do this too and how.

Is doing what you love day in and day out something within your reach? It most likely is. But, you will need to move beyond all kinds of doubts and fears disguised as questions. I made a shortlist of questions many people (and you too) have before they can actually do what they love most. Here are a few of those questions:

Do I have to be rich to live the life of my dreams?
No you don't. I, myself, am not from a wealthy family and I always had jobs during my college life. I do not have an Uncle Scrooge and you don't need one either.

Do I need to resign from my job in order to do what I really love?

No, not necessarily. Depending on your comfort zone, you can take different steps in the direction of a life full of joy. From 'how can I create more time for myself' to 'how can I build a company to support the life of my dreams', you will find all the answers in this book.

Do I need to start travelling like you? I just want a bit more flexibility and freedom in my life.

Of course you don't need to start travelling the world. You have your own personal preferences and I have mine. For me, travelling is an important part of leading a fulfilling life, but it doesn't have to be the same for you. By all means do whatever you love to do!

Do I have to be a risk taker?

No. This book gives advice to those who barely dare to take risks but also to those who want to burn all their bridges tomorrow while shouting 'Go to hell' to the entire world. And to everybody else in between.

Is this kind of lifestyle not just for twenty-somethings without any responsibilities or obligations?

No. This book is for everyone who is tired of following the predefined path. By the way, I was in my thirties when I started to walk my own path towards the life of my dreams.

When are you going to stop travelling and settle down?

When I am tired of travelling and when I feel like it. What does 'settling down' mean, anyway? Is there a definition and, if yes, can you explain it to me? Does it mean having a house, with a garden, a steady relationship, a fulltime job? If so, then here's my reply: been there, done that! It was nice and now it's time for something else. Settling down is not the Promised Land to me. Unless you are settling down in the Promised Land, of course.

What you do is impossible with kids, isn't it?

If you mean that you cannot take your kids with you to travel the world, then I would recommend googling 'how to travel with kids long-term' or 'nomadic families'. You will find plenty of families who are travelling the world as we speak. If you mean that YOU couldn't do so with YOUR kids, then that is a personal belief you're holding on to. If you mean that I live an irresponsible life which can't be done with kids, my answer is that nothing demands more responsibility than creating the ultimate freedom for oneself.

I would like to do what you do, but I cannot burn all my bridges, leave everything that I have built up behind and throw it away, can I?

Amused smile. No, I wouldn't advise you to do that. But it's not because you take a new, more fulfilling direction in life that you 'throw it all away'. It sounds a lot like 'worst case scenario thinking'. I write about this in the third chapter of this book, so please read on.

How can I live a comfortable life while earning less money?

Read the chapter about 'Necessary Money' and 'Fun Money' in this book. You will discover what the difference is between the two and how you can manage both.

Do I need to have a university degree or be a genius to live the life of my dreams?

No. Universities do not intend to teach you how to live a fulfilling life, quite the contrary.

Are you never tired of travelling?

Are you ever tired of doing the things you love doing?

MY BIGGEST FEAR WHEN I WAS WRITING THIS BOOK

"Annelies, I think my own book is very boring. Is this normal?"

It's Tuesday, 29 March 2016. I'm sitting crouched up in my writer's cave in Fuerteventura. The view is breath-taking: a reddish volcano, a cactus dangerously bending in the wind, mountains and a few waving palm trees. It turned out to be a fantastic decision to come here to write my book. The volcanic Canary Islands are a true energy bomb and a source of creative inspiration day in and day out. Some days, I am convinced that I am writing the best book ever. And then there are the days - and they outnumber the good ones - when I want to throw this rubbish manuscript in a deep dark hole. My writing coach Annelies says this is utterly normal. By using the word 'utterly' she makes me panic even more. I prefer to use the predictable and boring 'totally'. The word utterly doesn't even come to my mind. I am not an author. I cannot write. I don't know how to write. And really, which author considers his or her own book to be boring, anyway?

In order to get me back on track, Annelies asks me why I am writing this book, because somewhere on a plane between Berlin and Tenerife I seem to have forgotten. Via Messenger she explains what she would like to know from me, as a reader: "How the hell can you go surfing every day while I am answering messages in the middle of the night because I didn't have time during the day" She ends her message with a smiley. Then comes my smiley. I know she is right.

But in fact I am just scared to end up with a book that is only a half-hearted copy of 'The 4-Hour Work Week' by Timothy Ferriss. Five years earlier, that book turned my world upside down and it's one of the reasons I ended up here in Fuerteventura and not in a stuffy carpeted office with tasteless coffee somewhere in a provincial town. That book is the reason that I no longer have to respond to messages in the middle of the night like a lunatic. Today I am living my life instead of being lived.

And then I realise that I will never be able to write a book like Tim Ferriss has done. I am not an alpha man, nor a Silicon Valley wizzkid, nor a millionaire, nor a neurotic. I am a simple Belgian woman in her thirties, but with a slightly odd kind of lifestyle. Every morning I get up without an alarm clock, with only one thing on my mind: 'What would I love to do most today?' This has been my life since 2012. I live everywhere and nowhere and I lead a nomadic life which brought me to over 40 countries. And just in case you are wondering: I am not a millionaire, I do not have a sugar daddy and I never inherited anything. I simply became my own boss. This allowed me to discover how amazing it feels to no longer choose the life that others think I should lead, but to lead the life of my choice.

I have chosen the path that I really want to walk in this life. Annelies (and you too) would probably like to know 'how the hell' I did this. So that is what this book is all about.

CHAPTER 1

DOING WHAT IS
EXPECTED OF YOU IS
VERY COMFORTABLE.

UNTIL THE ALARM CLOCK
GOES OFF AND YOU HAVE
NO IDEA WHAT TIME IT
ACTUALLY IS.

MY LIFE AS IT IS: BY THE BOOK AND PERFECT.

July 2010, the last day of the Gentse Feesten, a 10-days festival in my hometown of Ghent. Sometime in the late afternoon I crawl out of bed and stumble to the bathroom. In the mirror I can see that nine days of non-stop partying have taken a heavy toll. I inspect the dark circles under my eyes. I bend forward towards the mirror and suddenly I cannot move my neck anymore. The pain is so strong I almost faint. After a night loaded with excruciating pain, my loving partner drives me to the emergency medical service. The diagnosis? A slipped disk. I am sent home with a bandage around my neck, multiple boxes of muscle relaxants and the advice to go see a specialist. The latter says: "A classic case of stress. Stress which fixes itself on the spine and has a special effect on the fourth neck vertebra." The chiropractor wrenches me in all kinds of positions. I return home relieved and happy as a child because I can move again. What I don't know then, is that I will see him again the next month. And the next. And almost every month in the next 2 years. Every time he gets me on the move again. With thousands of patients just like me, he has seen it all before. He repeats the same mantra over and over again: "You should reduce your stress levels and work less." I nod. It goes in one ear, out the other. He knows I don't really pay attention. I prefer to spend my well-earned money on emergency health repairs rather than adapting my lifestyle. Why would I change anything, anyway? I have a goal in mind...

Sailing around the world. Or playing a game of golf, in a place where the sun is always shining. Do what we love every single day. Enjoy life. Not when we are sixty-five, but preferably before we turn fifty. My life has a clear goal and waiting for the legal age of retirement is not part of it. I earn money and I am ambitious enough to be able to dream of an early retirement. Let's work really hard for the next fifteen years, so we can fully enjoy all the good things in life after that. If I need to put my health at risk during the next fifteen years I will cheerfully do so. How long is fifteen years in the global scheme of things, really?

Even if I wanted to, I really wouldn't know how to reduce the stress in my life. I am flying high at the moment. I am 'doing great', as we call it. My company Morpheus, only a start-up, is doing well. I turn over 200K euros in my first year. I have an office, an employee, freelancers, a pension plan, a nice car and applause from more senior entrepreneurs. I am working like a machine and the nice rewards feed my ambition even more. I am on a train which goes faster and faster. For the first time in my career, I earn what I was always entitled to, so it seems. And for the first time in my life, I feel like everything goes as I always dreamt it. I live with the man I want to grow old with, I go on comfortable all-inclusive holidays every year and when shopping, I use my credit card without worrying whether there is enough money in my account. I have a lovely apartment, totally designed the way I like it and I have nice friends who come over for tapas nights with lots of wine. We play tennis during the week and we dance the night away at the weekend. Work hard, play hard. That is what my life has become and the future seems bright. It is awesome.

> **66** *Life is what happens when*
> *you are busy making other plans.* **99**
> *John Lennon*

Until that particular day in 2011. The day my dreams shatter. A Sunday in August. He leaves. The man I want to grow old with. He leaves because he can't do it anymore. He leaves, because he tried long enough. Without understanding, I ask what 'he tried' exactly? "To make our relationship work", he says. I don't get it. He turns silent. I put my hand on his arm but he pushes it away. It's over. His bags are packed and are waiting at the door. I am left behind, totally shocked. I remain in shock the week after, the next month, the rest of the year. My foundations have been smashed to pieces and I have no clue how to pull my life back together. Was I that focused on our future that I didn't realise what a disaster the present was? Did my career and this damned early retirement blind me so much that I didn't see what was happening in front of my very own eyes?

A month later, I leave for France. A holiday that we both fantasised about just weeks before but which I spend alone now, in a double bed. Out of the blue my life has turned into hell and I have absolutely no idea how this happened. My French travel budget is spent on tissues instead of juicy barbecue meat. After one week I am back home in Ghent. An empty apartment which no longer feels like a home and Ikea chairs in cardboard boxes are waiting for me. I get them out, take off the plastic foil and start putting the screws in. Every turn of the screw makes me cry harder. What the hell has happened? How is it possible that only last month I was 'living the dream' and today I am putting together these bloody chairs? I start hyperventilating. My heart aches so much that I collapse and suddenly understand the term heartbroken.

There on my knees, facing those stupid chairs in false leather and with a screwdriver in my hand, I realise my life will never be the same again.

And that will eventually turn out to be a really good thing.

LIFE'S WAKE-UP CALL AND HOW TO SUCCESFULLY IGNORE IT: RUN FAST AND FAR AWAY.

"Please, please, please! Let the ferry reach the other side" I beg in silence.

It is hot on deck, especially in a taxi without aircon. The 9 hour flight has made my skin clammy and my face pale. I turn down the window for some fresh air, but my nose gets hit by the smell of diesel mixed with stale sweat. I close my eyes and try to erase the image of the hundreds of people around me, packed together likes sardines in a tin. Would the German engineer who made the strength calculations for this ferry also have taken this kind of scenario into account? My eyes remain closed as I try to recognise the noises surrounding me. I hear a rooster crow. I hear infectious laughter. A woman starts humming and almost immediately it turns into singing. I hear multiple women's voices, somebody starts to drum a beat. "Do you want a Fanta, miss?" I look up, aghast. A vendor is smiling from ear to ear and holds a bottle in front of my nose. It's tall and small without a label but it has the white letters written directly on the bottle. The content is fluorescent orange. I know this Fanta does not taste the same as the Belgian one. This one is sugary sweet and screams "Diabetes! Diabetes". I haven't exchanged my euros yet but the taxi driver doesn't mind paying for my drink. Together, we sip our bottles. I smile and remember why I chose to come to Kenya. It feels safe... I know what the Fanta tastes like here, the noises and the smells are familiar, I've felt the same dry heat on my skin years ago. Kenya feels like known territory. And that is exactly what I am looking for in this post-break-up period.

I DIED FIVE YEARS AGO. ONLY I DIDN'T REALISE IT BACK THEN.

Even though Kenya may feel like known territory, reality hits me hard in the face: somewhere between graduating in 2003 and this post-break-up trip in 2011, I have completely forgotten who I really am. Or maybe I have never known. However, the facts are simple: "My name is Lien De Pau. I was born on a Monday in May and I celebrated my 30th birthday a couple of months ago. Even though I spent the first years of my life in a village, I grew up in another province. This resulted in a schizophrenic accent for the rest of my life. Santa Claus brought me a handmade Barbie doll house which fitted perfectly under the slanted roof of my room. It was finished with wallpaper and carpet that looked suspiciously like the one in my grandparents' living room. He also brought me a work station with a hammer, a hand saw and a chisel. I seem to get on quite well with these building tools, so I enrol in a school which gets me ready for an engineering qualification. I finish my studies with flying colours. As of now, I can write Industrial Engineer on my business cards and this comes in handy, because on the night I am officially graduating I've also got my first working day out of the way. My career accelerates and flashes like lightning, including the expected burn-out at the age of 24. I get a new international job at 25 and in less than 3 years' time I have reached a high position with a lengthy job title reflecting its importance. Before my Icarus wings melt, I decide to run away and do what had been written in the stars for a long time: I become self-employed."

A self-employed boss lying on a beach in Kenya, that is. With an all-consuming, gaping hole in my soul. I am here looking for the strength and the motivation to get my life back on track and to pretend nothing happened. Which place could be more perfect than a white sandy beach, waving palm trees and turquoise tropical waters to do some self-reflection?

In fact it turns out that any place could be better. Because no matter how much coconut water I sip, I cannot find an answer to the ever returning nagging question: "what do I really want in my life?", no matter how desperately I am looking for the answer.

EVEN WHEN YOU TOTALLY HIT ROCK-BOTTOM, YOU CAN ALWAYS CHOOSE SOMETHING ELSE.

If you have always done what people expect you to do and what everyone else around you is doing, which answer can you possibly come up with to the question of what makes your heart beat faster? None. Or nothing near the truth. I can't come up with more than: "If you can do something, why wouldn't you want it?"

"IF YOU HAVE ALWAYS DONE WHAT WHAT EVERYONE ELSE IS DOING, WHICH ANSWER CAN YOU POSSIBLY COME UP WITH TO THE QUESTION OF WHAT MAKES YOUR HEART BEAT FASTER? NONE."

No matter how hard I try in Kenya, I can't come up with a satisfying answer. Simply because I never ever asked myself a question like that before. Or dared to ask myself it. Because just imagine that the answer is that I want to do something completely different than what I do today? Or suppose the answer is that I have absolutely no clue what I want in the months to come?

> **"Many people die at 25 and aren't buried until they are 75."**
> *Benjamin Franklin*

No matter how bad I feel, I prefer to avoid the hard confrontation with myself. So I eagerly grab every distraction as if it's the last rescue helicopter in a war zone. That's why I spend my days with the Kennaways sisters, the operators of the hotel where I am staying. Olivia and Lindsay chase baboons in the morning so that they cannot steal my toast. Apart from the daily protection of my breakfast, I also get my PADI Open Water Diving License. A small miracle, because I even panic in the swimming pool. Between my ever first practice dives I have to throw up. My instructor simply says: "We will see many fish now".

The dozens of books I brought with me to Kenya keep me busy as well. All of this allows me to keep on avoiding 'The Nagging Question'. I brought a book that my first boss recommended to me when I didn't know what to answer to his question "What do you want to do in life?" Oh irony. I am stuck in the chapter where Stephen Covey, the author of 'The 7 habits of highly effective people' writes that you should never forget that as a human being you always have choices. Every person always has the possibility to choose between different options. The choice to keep on doing what you always did, or the option to choose something else if you want. But the choice is always yours.

It resonates with me. Here on the beach in Kenya I realise that I have kept very few options open in my life and that therefore I feel stuck in it. I got stuck in a self-created nightmare full of obligations.

But the thought that there might be a tiny chance that I could choose something else than the disaster my life is at this moment, is a straw I clutch at. Even if I don't know yet what that 'something else' is. I cling to the idea of choice as if it is my last life line: "You always have choices, Lien", I repeat to myself night after night in my Kenyan bed.

"BUT WHAT DO I WANT THEN?" I WANT A LESS VAGUE QUESTION!

I leave Kenya without an answer to The Nagging Question "What do I really want to do with my life?" but with the strong conviction that I can choose another life over the one I am leading right now. And that belief is a first step in the right direction. The next step is to think of what that 'other' life will be. Simple, isn't it?

Well, no.

THE NEXT STEP IS TO THINK OF WHAT THAT 'OTHER' LIFE WILL BE. SIMPLE, ISN'T IT? WELL, NO.

I simply don't want to be who I am and do what I do anymore. But that is not really 'another' choice. It is only the opposite of who I am today and what I do today. Unfortunately you can't really work from there. It's like saying you don't want to eat spaghetti anymore, but it does not tell you yet what you would like to eat instead.

What I don't realise yet is that the question "What do I want to do with my life?" is the wrong question to ask. It is a trap, a tricky trap. It is the kind of question that makes you permanently chase your tail, turn around in hundreds of circles until you drop dead-tired and you are wondering why the hell you started turning in circles two hours ago. If you are looking for the kind of clarity that you can actually work with - like I did in Kenya - don't ask yourself such a vague question. Ask yourself the much more specific question "What do I want to do with my life today and in the next 6 months?"

HAVING MANY OPTIONS BUT NOT KNOWING WHAT YOU WANT: WRITE YOUR PERSONAL WHAT-I-WANT MANIFESTO.

Just when I try to find an answer to the more specific question "What do I want to do with my life today and the next 6 months?" another book comes my way. This one seems to contain exactly the help I need. In 'The 4-Hour Work Week', the author Tim Ferris describes how he discovered what he wants. His dreamlining technique could help me to take my first steps in my quest of what I really want to do with my life. Full of hope, I take a big sheet of white paper and draw 3 columns. Every column for a 'What-I-Want' list, each with a time-span of maximum 6 months:

- ❖ What I want to HAVE
- ❖ What I want to BE
- ❖ What I want to DO

So, shortly after my trip to Kenya, I decide to apply Tim's technique for the first time. After all, what do I have to lose?

The result is... erm, interesting?

I know you are dying to read my somewhat embarrassing What-I-Want Manifesto but before I reveal it to you, I want you to write a first draft of your own.

HAVE

BE

MY WHAT-I-WANT MANIFESTO

Really, first do this exercise. My What-I-Want Manifesto is not that embarrassing after all.

Okay, here we go...

The column What-I-Want-To-Have is quite full, with amongst many others, an Audi A5 Convertible. The whole column is packed with material stuff. Apparently I am a material girl with an unquenchable hunger. I am a bit embarrassed, but according to Tim there is no need to be: "It is very normal if you have defined your identity based on all the things you possess".

In the column What-I-Want-To-Be, there is only one wish. And it is written in small letters, in very bad, scrawled, almost unreadable handwriting: 'Being Happy'. That is what I truly want to be. But happiness has been lost to me for a very long time and I just don't know how to become happy again. This makes me despair even more.

And what I mentioned in my What-I-Want-To-Do column? If I tell you that it's 'do something to earn money and get even more stuff' then I am being very honest with you. And also a bit embarrassed. The content of my What-I-Want Manifesto is actually painfully materialistic. But, a pat on the back, at least I have been honest.

What else did I write down? Take four weeks of holiday next year. Not one or two weeks, but a complete month to try to feel happy again.

"BUT I WANT PASSION! MEANING! AND A CALLING!" THE REALITY.

Let's face reality... Making a manifesto of what you want to have/be/do, does not necessarily mean that you will immediately lead a life full of meaning or that you will find your true calling. Even though I was looking very hard for it, I didn't get the answer served on a plate.

But my intentions with this first What-I-Want Manifesto were sincere and it was the only straw I could cling to in order to get to know myself better. I had chosen the content of these lists myself, so I would also try to make everything come true that was on it. This way, I would be able to ascertain what the hopefully positive effect would be on this yawning black hole in my soul. I had no idea whether it would work, but it was the only tangible plan I had after months of trying to discover what I really wanted to do with my life. Sometimes it is better to keep on stumbling and trying to play the cards you are dealt. Especially when you are about to lose the game.

> "SOMETIMES IT IS BETTER TO TRY TO PLAY THE CARDS YOU ARE DEALT. ESPECIALLY WHEN YOU ARE ABOUT TO LOSE THE GAME."

After six months and having ticked off most of the items on my first What-I-Want Manifesto, I was still stuck with that empty feeling. It only confirmed how unconsciously I had been living my life until then. I did what people expected me to do without a lot of questioning and my first What-I-Want Manifesto was a reflection of this. No Audi A5 Convertible or four weeks holiday could solve that.

> **Don't feel guilty when you don't know what you want to do with your life. The most interesting people I know didn't know at 22 what they wanted to do with their lives. Some of the most interesting 40-year-olds I know still don't.**
> *Baz Luhrmann*

But what this first clumsy attempt led to was that, with every box I ticked, I got to know more about myself and what I wanted. And what I didn't want ANY LONGER... I didn't want a car anymore. I didn't want to own a house anymore. In fact, I almost didn't want to keep anything at all. I also didn't want to BE many things anymore: I didn't want to be stressed out all day, I didn't want to be unhappy and I didn't want to be the perfect friend-daughter-cousin-boss-entrepreneur anymore.

Thanks to this first What-I-Want Manifesto, I very slowly stepped away from my I-am-just-doing-something life towards a more conscious life. I moved closer towards the honest answer to my question: "What do I really want to do with my life?"

After all that box ticking during the spring of 2012, only one thing I really wanted to do remained on the list. Something that I absolutely wanted to do in the coming months: taking four weeks of holidays. So I booked a plane flight to a country that I'd never heard of, never mind being able to pinpoint it on a map. A country that would throw my life upside down to the extent that it entirely changed its direction: Malaysia.

CHAPTER 2

DO NOT MAKE IT
WORSE. STOP RUNNING
AIMLESSLY THROUGH
YOUR LIFE.

NOW.

"BUT WHAT DO I WANT?" I WANT TO HAVE A PANIC ATTACK IN A HINDU TEMPLE.

October 2012. I am completely disorientated. I don't recognise a single smell. I hear sounds that are completely unfamiliar to me. I see people of all colours and shapes but nobody looks like me. Everything is different. This was to be expected some 10.000 km south-east of my home country Belgium. It is boiling hot. Combined with the humidity level of a Turkish steam bath, the temperature here in Malaysia is unbearable. It forces me, dizzy and bathed in sweat, to sit down on the cold tiles of a Hindu temple. The only thing that is going through my mind is: "what the hell did I get myself into?"

I can't find my way, I don't know anyone around here. Imagine something happens to me... Nobody knows where I am, I barely know it myself. I frantically look for the street name 'Jalan Sehala' on my city map, without finding it anywhere. It takes a few more days, after encountering several more 'Jalan Sehalas' in Kuala Lumpur, when somebody tells me that Jalan Sehala simply means 'One-way street'.

The best thing I can come up with to try and cope with my disorientation is hiding in my bed, cocooned in the sheets. I wake up 26 hours later, completely groggy. I pull myself together and decide to explore the area around the hotel. In the meantime it is already evening. Or it is evening again. I lost track. My hotel is located in the busiest night life district of Kuala Lumpur, the area where everyone goes out for food at least once a week. There is smoke from the satay stalls everywhere, the ray fish are swimming in neon-lit aquariums waiting to be thrown on the grill, touters are waving their menus about in Malaysian, English and Mandarin, steaming hot noodle soup is served in big bowls and my eyes are drinking everything in. Never before have I seen such fantastic chaos, the chaos which is so typical for Malaysia and a lot of places in Asia. Despite having visions of how my body will cope with the unknown bacteria, I order soup (Soup is boiling. Boiling is good. Boiling kills bacteria), an ice cold beer (from the bottle and after having wiped the neck with a napkin) and fresh exotic fruits on a skewer for dessert. My guide-for-the-scared-white-tourist fiercely tries to dissuade me to eat the latter, but my eyes are bigger than my fear of acute traveller's diarrhoea. Exhausted from all the impressions, I head back to the hotel and sleep off my jetlag. A night and a day go by. My initial panic starts to take on manageable proportions and I am beginning to enjoy more and more my first days as a solo traveller in a country which was unknown to me until now. I head to a spa where fish nibble the skin off my feet, a character test for those who cannot stand being tickled. I celebrate my newly discovered freedom by tasting things that I assume are edible but with names I don't understand. I start to feel more comfortable in the chaos, the heat, that other world. I feel self-assured enough to leave Kuala Lumpur the day after and to tick off the last remaining box on my very first What-I-Want Manifesto. A few months ago I wrote down that I wanted to take 4 weeks off from work and take a long holiday. So now the time has come and I am kicking off this What-I-Want trip with a visit to the city of Melakka. Melakka is a UNESCO World Heritage site, just like Bruges in Belgium. But it has noodles instead of fries with mayonnaise.

No less than 24 hours later I am drifting from left to right through the streets of Melakka. Luckily for me there are no policemen around, because drunkenness – and definitely in public – is not really appreciated in Malaysia. But even though I'm not walking in a particularly straight line, my blood actually contains zero percent of alcohol. The somewhat glazed-over look in my eyes is not the result of the beer I had, but of an innocent cup of … tea.

The morning had started off strangely from the word go. After a night of almost no sleep and a surprising conversation in Kuala Lumpur with a Flemish expat ("At least we still teach our kids values and behaviours. For example, they cannot slap the Filipina household help."), I crawl on a bus for a three hour journey in the direction of Melakka where I will find the foundations of Malaysia. In Melakka I start wandering about, because in fact I have no clue at all about what I want to do or see here. While I am walking around somebody beckons me into one of the alleyways to enter a - what later on would prove to be - a drinking cave. A Malaysian drinking cave that is. I mean a tea house. The owner of the teahouse has Chinese roots, but her name is Korean: "Pak, which means 'White'", she says. Mrs. White turns out to be an amazing hostess who introduces me to the joys of the Chinese tea ceremony. This is accompanied with a clear word of warning. "You could well be returning home drunk.' smiles Mrs White, "Yes, tea drunk. You can get drunk from drinking too much tea." Mrs. Pak obviously doesn't know I am from Belgium, the country where beer was invented, so I forgive her for worrying unnecessarily. After slurping tea for an hour I am chatting readily, I love the entire world, everybody is my friend and my self-confidence reaches incredible heights. I have just about enough control of my senses not to buy five kilos of superfluous tea before I drift out of her teahouse.

I walk along the river in the direction of Destination I Have No Clue. The fresh air performs miracles to my drunken head. Dusk is falling and the street lights along the path light up. A bit further on is a small harbour and I know that boats leave from there for a kitsch riverside trip which only exists to keep tourists entertained. Oh, why not? I buy a ticket and before even realising, I am on the Asian version of The Love Boat. Romance is in the air: the Western couples cuddle, the Chines tourists take thousands of selfies with their flashlights, chattering uninterruptedly while immediately posting the pictures on their version of Facebook.

> **BUT HERE ON THE LOVE BOAT IT HITS ME HARD IN THE FACE. "THIS IS IT. THIS IS WHERE I BELONG."**

Still a bit lightheaded because of my tea escapade I'm enjoying the cheesy music blasting out of the speakers, the sound of the flowy river, the hot oppressive air and the mouth-watering smells coming from the Peranakan restaurants on the river banks. And then this feeling washes over me. A feeling that I know. But it has been such a long time since I last felt it. In the past year there was no room for it because I was busy surviving stacks of pain and sadness, and gathering what was left of my dreams. But here on The Love Boat it hits me hard in the face. "This is it. This is where I belong. At this moment in my life. This is where I have to spend my time for now. This is what I have to do. This feels right, even though I have no idea why." For a couple of very long seconds I am happy. Incredibly happy.

BIGGER, CRAZIER, BETTER,... AND TOTALLY IMPOSSIBLE: MY WHAT-I-WANT MANIFESTO V2.0.

Have you ever had that feeling in your life when you were certain: 'This isn't just happening. This is happening for a reason. This had to happen.'? That night on The Love Boat in Melakka was such a moment. I knew it. I felt it. Looking back, this kitsch boat packed with cuddling tourists was a turning point in my life. That night would determine all of the most important decisions I would take the following year. Decisions which would turn my world upside down from a life-as-I-thought-it-had-to-be into a life-on-my-own-terms. A pre-Melakka-life and a post-Melakka-life.

> **❝Only put off until tomorrow what you are willing to die having left undone.❞**
> *Pablo Picasso*

There in Melakka I make my second What-I-Want Manifesto. A version 2.0. It is on a much bigger scale and with far bigger consequences than 'taking four weeks of holiday' which I wrote in my first manifesto a year earlier. In my new Manifesto, using a very faint pencil, almost impossible to read, I write: 'I want to travel forever'. I have no clue how I will be able to spend more time on the Asian side of the world. With a hectic life and a successful company in Belgium this seems totally ridiculous. But on the bus from Melakka to Penang I decide to not simply ignore this big, crazy and impossible idea that is also paired with butterflies in my belly. And all I can think is: It's not because an idea seems completely lunatic and unattainable, that it really is.

"IT'S NOT BECAUSE AN IDEA SEEMS COMPLETELY LUNATIC AND UNATTAINABLE, THAT IT REALLY IS."

Very soon I am hitting my next and third destination, Penang, which is an island situated on the west coast. It is the second biggest city in Malaysia and from a political point of view it follows its very own course. This is something you notice in the daily life because more than anywhere else a mixture of nationalities and religions reigns here. But most of all, Penang turns out to be – and I am putting it rather mildly– an enemy to my stretchy pants.

According to my guide book Penang is a real paradise for culture and history lovers, but all inhabitants seem to share another favourite pastime... eating. As it happens it is also one of my favourite activities. Aromatic bowls full of steaming soup, crispy bites wrapped in newspaper, BBQs covered with perfectly roasted meat, plastic bags filled to the brim with freshly squeezed fruit juice. I walk past one tempting obstacle after another.

To a Penangite eating is like breathing: a lifesaving activity which you have to do continuously. Either they've just had something to eat or they are eating as we speak, or they are on their way to have food. Every dish also has 'its' restaurant: you can eat the best Char Koay Teow in Chulia Street (not my personal favorite by the way) and for the most refreshing Cendol you head for Penang Road. Fortunately it appears not to be too complicated to discover the favourite spots of the Penangites. They are so proud of their food heritage that these spots are not kept secret for tourists. After a few days in town I discover the most successful approach to get to know the best food stalls. Everything starts with acting like a tourist who has lost the way. A role that I play with much fervour, since most of the time I have no idea where I am anyway. My unsuspecting victim is usually a local passer-by who pities a confused-looking tourist. Since the helpful Penangite has likely just had lunch, is eating at the time or is heading for food somewhere, I can easily steer the conversation to all things food. "Do you know where Jalan Burma is? I heard the best Hokkien Mee of the island can be found over there." And then I get the magical answer I am looking for "Yes, it is very good indeed. But the one on Lebuh Carnavon is even better!" followed by the full explanation of why the noodles in Lebuh Carnavon should be considered the best. Then I get asked the most common question in Malaysia: "Sudah makan?" which means as much as "Have you already eaten?" Although my belly is stuffed to the brim with food I can only answer "No I haven't eaten yet". Right away I get an invitation to go there and taste the noodles together. At one point I become so adept at this kind of conversation that I can easily eat five, six, seven times per day with a table companion I would only have known for less than five minutes. A taxi driver once brought me to his favourite Nasi Kandar restaurant where we enjoyed finger-licking curries together after he picked me up at the airport one morning. And I remember one evening at 2 o'clock in the morning after a night out in a pub with my friend Jesse, where I ended up in his favourite stall to eat the best noodle soup of the island, only to be whisked away by car the next morning by my friend Karen for a more than one hour long drive to eat Curry Mee at The Two Sisters. These sisters are living legends. Every single day (except with Chinese New Year), for over 60 years, this flavourful soup is being freshly prepared and served by two very, very old aunties. No need to say that as a food addict I am having the time of my life in Penang. My almost illegibly and in very faint pencil written 'I want to travel forever' is completed by 'and put more of that delicious food in my mouth'.

THE NOT-TO-BE-IGNORED URGE IN ALL OF US: THE WILL TO DISCOVER WHY WE ARE HERE ON THIS EARTH.

It is a sticky, subtropical night in Penang and I've just said my farewells to Joyce after we finished a bottle of wine in the wonderful Renitang heritage hotel where I am staying. Joyce is a lot of fantastic things, amongst which a heavy fan of audiobooks and podcasts. Her love for podcasts is really infectious and that same evening in bed I discover by chance the podcast 'Personal Development for Smart People' by Steve Pavlina. Inspired by 'Star Trek: The Next Generation', Steve strives for a life without a job but all the more satisfaction. In the description of one of his podcasts I read: "How do you discover your real purpose in life? I'm not talking about your job, your daily responsibilities, or even your long-term goals. I mean the real reason why you're here at all – the very reason you exist." It is not the description I find intriguing. I have seen, read and heard it in hundreds of versions. It is the exercise he suggests: practical, short and powerful. If it turns out not to work for me, I would have wasted one hour of my life at the most. "And when I am finished I will get to know why I am here on this earth? Okay!" Steve's approach consists of four steps and it is like a What-I-Want Manifesto on steroids! It is kind of a What-I-Must-Do Manifesto. According to Steve I am only four simple steps away of finding my mission in life and here they are:

1. Take a piece of paper or open a new document on your PC (this is what I did, because I can type faster than I write by hand).

2. On top of the page, write "What is the real purpose of my life?"

3. Write an answer, any answer that pops up in your head. It doesn't need to be a full sentence. A few words are just fine.

4. Repeat the third step until you write an answer which makes you cry. That is your true mission, THE reason why you are on this earth.

Yep, UNTIL YOU START CRYING. You read it correctly.

Just like Tim Ferriss assured me a few years before that it was okay that my What-I-Want Manifesto contained mostly material things, Steve Pavlina assures me during this exercise that "the more you lead an unconscious I-do-whatever kind of life, the harder the exercise will be and the more iterations of step 3 you will need. Some people are ready in only 50 iterations, others need 500." When I complete the exercise in my bed in Penang I have to repeat the third step 87 times. And at the end I don't start crying. But the moment I write it down I know damn well: 'This is it!' Fifteen more answers follow, but I already know that I have found it... my purpose, my passion, the meaning of my life, the reason why I am here on this earth.

> **66The two most important days of your life are the day you were born and the day you find out why.99**
> *Mark Twain*

That night I realise that the second edition of my What-I-Want manifesto in which it says that 'I want to travel forever', is ready for an immediate upgrade. While my first manifesto was a slow experiment of trial & error spread out over more than six months, Steve's exercise has an immediate impact. The morning after I change my job title on LinkedIn and adjust my e-mail signature to reflect my mission. But on the same day a long term process is kicking off... I will start using my discovered mission as a compass to take massively important decisions about my life.

SHOULD VERSUS MUST: FROM MY WHAT-I-WANT MANIFESTO TO DISCOVERING WHAT-I-MUST-DO

In our lives there are a lot of things we think we 'should' do. Do mind the number of times you mention the word. "You should read that book!" Since I read Stephen Covey for the first time back in 2004 I try to scrap 'should' from my vocabulary. Sometimes I have a slip of the tongue and say "Hey, you should do this-or-that" but almost immediately I continue "No, in fact, you don't have to do anything". Almost every 'should' in our life is a consequence of how other people want us to lead our life.

It can be small and even nice things (like the book suggestion), but they can also be paralysing things. The author Elle Luna describes this beautifully in her book called 'The Crossroads of Should and Must': "Shoulds are highly influential systems of thoughts that pressure us." The what-is-expected-of-me-should, so to speak. If you choose to lead a life full of these kinds of should, you choose to lead someone else's life instead of your own. You choose to do what other people think you should do. You choose to take the easy road. Doing this has two major advantages: your path will be quite smooth, without all too many obstacles and people will love you for doing as they please.

> **"Tried to run from it.**
> **Tried to hide.**
> **Tried to put it on a train.**
> **Kicked and smacked it with a blunt shovel.**
> **Tried to write it off in a big refrain.**
> **To this day it hasn't gone away,**
> **it hasn't gone away."**
> Triggerfinger

But then there is also that other 'should'. The should which is actually a 'must'. Something deep down inside yourself. A must which makes you do, create and build things. Because you can't do otherwise. A must never accepts compromises. It is that must which you have tried to bury under a stone for many years, but which always comes back knocking at your door. This must reflects who you really are, what you believe in and what you stand for. It is a reflection of your most authentic you. Elle Luna describes it as follows: "Must is when we stop conforming to other people's ideals and start connecting to our own – and this allows us to cultivate our full potential as individuals." This must is constantly tempting you to leave the path which is paved with the expectations of those around you. This must seduces you onto a new exciting path. A path which has already been walked by thousands of others before you, but which is completely unknown and unique to you. You don't have a road map, you don't even know if this path leads somewhere. It is packed with obstacles, hard work and doubts. There is no guarantee for success. But it is something you MUST do. Without compromise. Without negotiation.

"THERE IS NO GUARANTEE FOR SUCCESS"

The funny thing is that I have always known my must. It was buried deep down inside me but I never managed to really define it clearly. Thanks to Steve Pavlina's exercise I rediscovered my must and found a way to describe it in just a few words. I finally succeeded that night in Penang and it has made my life easier, more efficient and more productive. I test every opportunity, every offer coming my way, every pitch I receive, every chance passing by, to my must. "Is this going to help me live my mission more or will it divert me from fulfilling my must?" is the question I constantly ask myself, for both the day to day decisions and the life decisions I have to make. Thanks to this simple question I can say no more often, more consistently and with more comfort and confidence. I am hardly ever tempted to say yes. So when I end up saying yes to something, it is because it is a Hell Yeah!

> **"If you are not saying 'Hell Yeah' about something, say 'No'."**
> Derek Sivers

During that subtropical night in Penang in which I realise that my What-I-Want Manifesto v2.0 needed an unprecedented upgrade so it can become a What-I-Must-Do, I also realise that there is no way back. The future will look substantially different, because I will say Yes to my mission and No to everything else. It has made my life more meaningful, more honest and more real. That is why I want to share Steve Pavlina's exercise with you: so you can get real about your life too.

THE VERY REASON WHY I EXIST

You probably wonder what my must is. Do you really want to know?

I am an 'Explorer of Life'.

I get my energy from the discoveries I make. Those discoveries can come as marvellous people I get to know, unimaginable places I visit and new knowledge I absorb. Being an explorer is my must. It is who I am and the reason why I am on this earth. I can't do otherwise. I am 'Lien The Explorer'.

"But how the hell are you going to pay your way with this?" a little voice inside my head piped up.

CHAPTER 3

CHOOSE YOUR OWN PATH
AND EXPECT A LOT OF
CRITICISM.

MAINLY FROM YOURSELF.

We all have a purpose being on this planet.

But it's up to every single one of us to do something with that purpose. Or not.

"WHAT MAY I WISH YOU THIS YEAR?" A LOT OF DRAMA PLEASE!

Finally discovering your mission in life is a great feeling. It feels like a relief. As if all the pieces of your life's puzzle fall into place. Once you know what you really love to do (to write, to raise kids, to be a doctor or to be an Explorer of Life like me) you won't be able to put it out of your head. Once you have discovered why you have been born and why you live on this planet, nothing remains the same. You just can't continue with your life like you did before and simply be happy with it. The discovery of your mission can be intimidating, fascinating and all-consuming. There is a before-the-discovery and an after-the-discovery. And this is exactly the reason why we avoid admitting to ourselves what we really love. That's why our mission is often hidden so deeply inside us, for months, years, sometimes even an entire lifetime.

When Annelies asks me "how the hell I manage to go surfing every day?" she is actually asking me not one but two questions. On the one hand she asks me for practical advice. For tips and tricks to organise her life in such a way that she can free up the maximum amount of time to do all those things she loves. Just like so many others she wants a piece of paper with instructions on working efficiently, time management, productivity hacks and the kind of advice you can implement as from tomorrow. However, the truth is that I can give you hundreds of tips, but none of them will help you any further. You can set yourself as many targets as you like, you can have as many sweet dreams as you want and you can download all the apps available for efficient time management, the truth is that you will return to slaving away at work tomorrow. Why? Because all this advice bypasses something you need even more than knowledge or skills when choosing a life in line with your mission. You need to have balls. Of steel.

Erm. No. Luckily you don't need those. But what is holding us back then?

When Annelies wonders how the hell I manage to go surfing every day the implicit question she is asking requires a far more complex answer than some practical time management tricks. She is asking me how I found the courage to start rebuilding my life so I can go surfing every day instead of driving to a dusty office every morning. Frankly, you will only lead a mission driven life if you find the courage to step off that beaten track you have been on for all your life. Besides courage to get you started, you will need lots of willpower not to return at the slightest setback you come across. Before I tell you where you can get that courage and that willpower, I need to explain a couple of things about human psychology and biology.

However much I would like it to be different, most of us will never bring about major changes in our lives. As humans we are just utterly bad at making the necessary changes. We are biologically programmed to teach ourselves a new skill and then repeat it over and over again until it has become a habit. Habits require far less energy than developing new skills. Everybody who learned how to drive a car knows this. In the early stages you are acutely aware of everything. But after years of experience you just drive on automatic pilot even when navigating through a busy city centre. Over the centuries, habits have proven to be key to our survival and they are therefore a marvellous example of evolution at its best. But they have one huge disadvantage. Habits are the enemies of change. Everybody who has ever tried to change their diet and every smoker who has ever attempted to quit cigarettes more than once knows this. Changing these habits requires doing what we biologically don't want to do: we need to break through those hard-earned habits which run on automatic pilot. And that is why it's so damn hard to make those necessary changes in order to live a more fulfilling life.

Research shows that breaking habits is something you only do if there is sufficient reason to. Hence the self-help books on how you can change your life for the better are turning into an ever-growing Still To Do list on your bookshelf. You'd rather be bored to death or be drowning in your own misery than cope with any kind of change. Even when you are stressed to the level of chronic panic attacks or you know deep down that the life you are living now is not the life you really want, the likelihood that you will make the necessary changes to start living your dream life after reading this book is almost zero. As long as the boredom or the pain is not boring or painful enough, you will calmly continue doing what you've always done... slowly proceeding towards the day you are going to die. Please don't think you are biologically different from me or anyone else on this planet.

"BREAKING HABITS IS SOMETHING WE ONLY DO IF THERE IS SUFFICIENT REASON TO."

The good news is that there are also a lot of people out there who find a way to dramatically turn their lives around despite biology working against them! They find a pretty damn good reason to make a change. If you spend a bit of time researching their inspiring stories you can quickly discover what was driving them to make these changes. It turns out that looking death straight into the eyes seems to have been a wake-up call for many of them: a traffic accident, a cancer diagnosis, a burn-out, getting fired, a devastating divorce, a seriously ill child... All these events made those people's foundations tremble to such an extent that they were the trigger for a massive change in their life. Most of the people who live through a dramatic event like this will say afterwards: "This was the best thing that could've ever happened to me." Similar dramatic events may give you the opportunity too to find the courage and the willpower to change your life. My own story described in this book also started with a dramatic event: the day I came home from my holiday in the Ardèche when I was on my knees facing those stupid chairs in fake leather, with a screwdriver in my hand and I realised that my life would never be the same again.

Of course I don't wish you lots of bad luck, but be aware that no other event has the same power to change your life than a dramatic wake-up call.

UNFORTUNATELY YOU ARE JUST NOT UNHAPPY ENOUGH TO MAKE THAT NECESSARY CHANGE.

If you have no clear wake-up call right now in your life, if you have no drama unfolding in front of your eyes as we speak, allow me to create some for you: when you enjoy a lovely night out with four of your best friends next weekend, you should realise that one of you will die before s/he reaches the retirement age. Have you ever thought about who it will be? Will it be your best friend Tim, who you have known since high school? Or maybe his amazing wife Marie, who just gave birth to their twins? Or maybe it is going to be your partner, or his brother? Have you ever realised it might as well be you? Don't assume that you will be among the lucky four to survive. Your chances are equally limited as those of your four best friends.

If you are lucky enough to reach your retirement age and live longer, you should know that almost everybody who is at the point of dying has regrets about what they did or did not do during their life. But research shows that almost everyone has one regret in common at the end of their lives: "That I didn't do what I really wanted to do". Most of us take all our dreams and all our potential into the grave with us. After my little drama back in 2011 I decided I didn't want to be like all those other people who die with regrets. I didn't want to be that coward who never found the courage to do what made my heart sing. I felt life was too short for that. And research shows it probably is.

> 66Your time is limited, so don't waste it living someone else's life.99
> Steve Jobs

Dramas are the strongest catalysts for change.

With the catch-phrase above I just gave you the key to a more meaningful life. Because if this year is going to be just like the last one, you — and only you — can create the trigger for the change that you have been longing for so much. If there is not going to be a drama for you this year I suggest you keep your eyes open for something in your life that can serve as that trigger for change. The key to change is in your own hands.

Although I had a huge trigger for change that night when I was crying on the floor in my lovely apartment, I also kept my eyes open for smaller, less dramatic events to keep the change-momentum going. Like that night on The Love Boat in Melakka when I whispered to myself: "This feels fantastic and I want more of this. Let me find a way to travel forever and experience this magical feeling over and over again". This event is not dramatic in itself and therefore not really a change trigger for my transition from work slave to surfer. But it is the fact that I do not let this moment pass by like an unimportant news item. I force myself to stand still and listen to the message which is given to me. I promise myself to act upon it. That makes the Melakka moment a positive catalyst for change. So when you are not living a big drama this year, try to find your Melakka moment, grab it with both hands and use it as a trigger to make those necessary changes you are craving for.

WARNING: FINDING YOUR TRIBE WILL ACCELERATE THE CHANGE.

During my last days in Penang the universe sends me a message. Okay, the opening sentence of this paragraph sounds like I am losing it a bit (but hey, 'being crazy never hurt anyone'). In only a few days' time I meet five people who, independently from each other, are living my dream of being an Explorer of Life. They all tell me: "I am not travelling. This is how I live." The first one is Fe. Or Fede. Or Federico. Part-time inventor and fulltime traveller. A handful of companies in his home country Argentina provide enough income to finance his lifestyle. A few hours after meeting Fe, I run into Celine and Xavier who give a photo presentation in the bar where I am sipping my iced coffee. They are a Swiss couple who have been travelling by bike since 2010. They have ended up in Penang for three months. Currently just the two of them, but shortly with a baby because Celine is in Penang to give birth. I ask her what it feels like to be travelling for 3 years. She smiles and her answer is as clear as spring water: "We don't travel, Lien. This is how we live. Being on the road is our life." That same evening the universe sends Brandon to my favourite and illegal watering hole in a dark backside alley of Penang. Brandon is American and – naturally – a fulltime optimist. Awesome! Amazing! Soooo nice! No idea where he gets his energy from. He leads his lifestyle company from the hostels he stays at. At midnight the watering hole closes and we continue our discussions on the wooden pier of the Tan Jetty. Charles, another American, a part-time sarcastic and a fulltime free spirit, joins us. It will be one of those nights every traveller needs to experience at least once during his or her trip. A mix of comradery, philosophy, new insights, self-reflection and also a bit of peeing your pants because of laughing too hard. That night we discuss all kinds of topics: we come up with a solution for the climate problem, the unequal division of wealth in the world and the far too short lifetime of a smartphone battery. All the typical discussions held by privileged middle class people in exotic destinations.

Our conversation is also about travelling, discovering the world and the phenomenon of digital nomads. Since the book 'The 4-Hour Work Week' by Tim Ferriss was published in 2007 a growing number of people are working from any location in the world, something I find particularly attractive as an 'Explorer of Life'. It doesn't matter where these digital nomads are in the world. They only need an internet connection to be able to work. "What is a traveller, what is a tourist and is there a difference with a nomad?" Charles asks. It is the kind of discussion you can only have in the middle of the night somewhere on a jetty in a foreign country. We agree pretty quickly that a tourist and a traveller always intend to return to the place they call 'home'. The moment of return can be just a week or 2 in the future in the case of a tourist or months and even years in the future in the case of a traveller. A nomad however considers the world her or his 'home' and has no intention to return home to lead a sedentary life there. "What are you, Brandon?" I ask him. "A nomad, that's for sure", he says. "And you, Charles?" "I'm a nomad too." "And you, Lien?" I'm hesitating. I am here in Penang as a tourist, that's for sure. Within 2 weeks, this Explorer of Life will fly back home. To Ghent, to my apartment, to 'home'.

Walking back to my hotel room I realise that these last days' encounters with Fe, with Celine and Xavier and with Brandon and Charles have opened a door to another world for me. A world where I know people who are living my crazy dream! People who already do what I would love to do. People who adopted the lifestyle I read about in 'The 4-Hour Work Week' a year before on a sandy beach in Kenya. A lifestyle of whom I thought: "Yeah right, sounds great to me, but not very realistic". All of a sudden my mission as an Explorer of Life seems to be within reach for completely normal people. Like me. At 3 o'clock in the morning my eyes open slowly and carefully and a small light is starting to light up. Would I really be able to achieve my personal mission to be an "Explorer of Life"?

> "WOULD I REALLY BE ABLE TO ACHIEVE MY PERSONAL MISSION TO BE AN "EXPLORER OF LIFE"?"

Without realising Charles and Brandon have succeeded to question the belief I had in my head that was telling me that "travelling for an indefinite period of time is a dream and all the more for normal and hardworking people like me". That night in Penang they show me that I can be an Explorer of Life if I really want to. For days afterwards the impact of their personal stories fully gets to me. "But wait. Imagine. Imagine that one day I would actually do what makes my heart sing? Imagine that living my mission of being an Explorer of Life wouldn't be a dream anymore but my actual life. Imagine this would be possible?!"

And then my head exploded!

My What-I-Want Manifesto based on Tim Ferriss' dreamlining technique had led to getting to know myself a lot better. It helped me to understand what I wanted to have, to do and to be (or not) in a short timespans of 6 months. The crying exercise by Steve Pavlina had led to finding my true mission. Now that I've suddenly realised that there were people who were fulfilling my mission and did what I loved to do too, my dream didn't seem so crazy anymore. Since that night in Penang I had role models to look up to, whom I could ask questions and who inspired me to take the next step and showed me how to do so. I am convinced that finding my tribe of people who already did what I would love to do most, has allowed me to take the next step in living my dream life.

So once you have discovered what your mission is (if not, quickly go back to the previous chapter) the next step is to look for people who are already doing what you love to do. Have you dreamed since childhood of living from your music? Then surround yourself with some professional musicians who play for everything they've got! Do you want to market your own ecological jewellery collection? Then look who is behind the most successful jewellery collections, contact them and listen to their story. Look for inspiring role models who realise their own mission and ask them how the hell they did it. Just like I did, use the knowledge of your tribe to inspire you to start walking on your own unique path and to think about ways you can live your dream life.

LIVING THE LIFE OF YOUR DREAMS? "YOU'RE JOKING, RIGHT?" SHE SAID.

For as long as I can remember I have been deeply convinced that travelling is something that cannot last forever. That travelling is not 'the real life'. Waking up every morning without an alarm clock and do what I love sounds like a magnificent dream which can be a reality for a little while, but which unfortunately doesn't last. Although I grew up in a family where travelling (even for long periods of time) is very common, I also grew up with the idea that travelling is something you do temporarily. The end of your trip is marked by the ever shrinking amount of money in your bank account. After your trip it's time to pick up 'the normal life of working', whether you want it or not. Even in my explorer family, travelling is not something you can do forever.

"Explorer of Life? That's not a real job, Lien! Going on a holiday forever? Impossible!"

My whole life this belief has created a permanent stream of never-ending songs put on endless repeat in my head. Like a stuck record they would say "This is impossible. You can't do this."

But since the Steve Pavlina exercise I've known that travelling and exploring are an inherent part of what I want to do in my life. That the 'Explorer of Life' inside me has to go travelling for a long time in order to be really satisfied and content. It's something I must do. I feel that in this nomadic lifestyle something is awaiting me and that there is something in it for me to discover. No idea what that could be. No idea how I will make money being an explorer. But I am willing to find out at all cost. No matter how many weeks, months or years it will take.

I realise there is only one thing that stops me from fulfilling my mission as an Explorer of Life. I am holding myself back. It's me, only me.

"I AM HOLDING MYSELF BACK. IT'S ME, ONLY ME."

The record in my head has been stuck for over 30 years on the same popular beliefs, with "You cannot do this!" as the number 1 of the hit parade. I have never really been aware of the recurring words, but they create a compelling chorus in my head. Even though these beliefs do not reflect reality at all, I listen to the words and I have been cheerfully singing along with them all my life. I obey and do whatever the songs tell me to do and what not to do. By doing this I unconsciously give those beliefs superpowers. I let them hold me back and limit my freedom. And I have been allowing them to do so all my life.

I'm sure that you too have strong beliefs about what you can and cannot do in your life. I am also convinced that you, just like me, have been listening all your life to your own unique hit parade of limiting beliefs and that you too have allowed them to hold you back from what you really love to do.

THE BIGGEST SHOWSTOPPER IN STARTING TO DO WHAT YOU LOVE.

Limiting beliefs have been pumped into our brains so badly that it doesn't even occur to us to question them. We don't even understand that we have the choice not to listen to them. Some people refer to those strong beliefs as 'the inner critic' or 'the little devil on your shoulder'. Whatever you like to call them, we should be aware that most of us have collected an extensive hit parade full of these beliefs. They are created from childhood onwards in our heads. First by our parents and our teachers. Later by the friends we have during our college life. Next by our partner and by our colleagues at work. The culture in which we grew up has a big influence on what we consider normal behaviour and what isn't. All these influences together create the framework in which you and I live, with written and unwritten rules. And far more often than the written rules, the unwritten ones in our society define how we live our lives and which choices we can and cannot make.

Although these limiting beliefs are holding us back to chase our dreams, there is a very good reason for why we have them going through our heads all the time. Listening to these beliefs is part of our instinct. This instinct of survival makes sure that we are safe, and stay safe. This instinct ensures we avoid as many physical and mental risks as possible: the pain of failure, the sadness of being rejected, the disappointment of not succeeding, and so on. My limiting belief "Travelling forever is a dream that isn't made for me" is there to warn me for all the bad stuff which might happen to me when I would try to fulfil this crazy dream. It ensures that I won't die poor (because how will you make a living!) and lonely (your family and friends back home will forget about you!). My belief protects me from all these horrible things which -for sure- will happen if I do this crazy thing! It constantly reminds me it is a bad idea to keep travelling forever.

> **66And does it make you feel good. Knowing that you could. Have power on me.99**
> *Katey B.*

Discovering which discouraging beliefs are in your head, how they affect your everyday life and how they limit your ability to do amazing things, brings you closer to the idea that you too can fulfil your mission if you really want to. Just like me, you have your hit parade of limiting beliefs. And I am wondering which ones are in your Top 3?

THERE IS NOT ONE LIMITING BELIEF BUT A COMPLETE HIT PARADE OF THEM.

"I can't do that."

"Everybody is going to laugh at me."

"I am not good enough."

"My kids will think that I've gone crazy."

"I am going to lose all my money."

"I am going to lose all my money AND be lonely."

"What if I lose all my money AND I am lonely AND everybody will laugh at me?"

> **I've been worryin' that
> my time is a little unclear.
> I've been worrying that
> I'm losing the ones I hold dear.
> I've been worrying that we all live our
> lives in the confines of fear.**
> Ben Howard

MY VERY OWN HIT PARADE OF DISA...

⭐ 1

② 2

③ 3

The flipside of our hit parade of limiting beliefs is that it's meant to protect us and it does that in a very convincing way. Our beliefs prevent us from taking unnecessary risks. That's why (at first sight) it looks as if these beliefs have the best intentions for our wellbeing.

But when you look at them in more detail you will see that these beliefs do not leave any room for nuance. They might sound like "I cannot do this" or "Everybody is going to laugh at me". These are not what we call nuanced expressions. There is no grey zone. There is not even a white one. All our beliefs are pitch black.

And wat is the result of our beliefs? We become paralysed. We come to a stand-still. Instead of moving forward, we do nothing. Even the slightest thought of doing something that might take us away from our current path makes us push the brakes. We put ourselves to a hold, unconsciously but fiercely. We tell ourselves "No, this dream is not for me". When we obey to our limiting beliefs we take fewer risks. And this can be a very good survival strategy.

The downside is that these beliefs don't care whether we lead a fulfilling and satisfying life. These beliefs are not interested in whether we contribute to the world in line with our biggest dreams. They are not interested in whether we fulfil our mission. The beliefs want to keep us on the safe side of life. They want to keep us on the path that everyone else paved for us, on the path where everybody else is and they lead us to a place where we do not necessary find most contentment.

THREE STRATEGIES TO DEAL WITH YOUR LIMITING BELIEFS. IGNORING IS NOT ONE OF THEM.

Wouldn't it be awesome if we could just switch off these beliefs, just like we can do with the radio? Absolutely! But unfortunately that's not how it works, no matter how hard you try. Your hit parade of limiting beliefs is on endless repeat and there is no stop button to be seen. So if we can't switch them off, how about we just ignore them? We pretend that they are not there and just live those dreams? Alas again! The strategy of ignoring is not very successful either. Our hit parade is written by the world's best songwriters, so every single one of them is an earworm. Once they are inside your head, you keep on singing along persistently, whether you want to or not. Hence turning off the beliefs in our heads or simply ignoring them are not effective strategies. Fortunately there are strategies that actually work and that can help you to cope with all those limiting beliefs inside your head. I use three different strategies and interchange them depending on the situation and the belief. I advise you to experiment with them too as a way to discover which one is the most effective one for you. I know from experience that dealing with limiting beliefs can take a lot of time: time to discover them, time to challenge them, time to rework them and time to let go of them. Having multiple strategies at hand to help you go through this intense process is key to the progress you will make.

The first strategy I use is one I learned by travelling a lot. I call it the "Unlikeliness Strategy": I realise that it is highly unlikely that the catastrophe described in one of my limiting beliefs will effectively become reality. When my limiting belief pops up telling me that I will end up under a bridge with no money, I ask myself the question "How likely is it that this worst case scenario will actually happen?" Then I come to realise that the chance that, amongst all the different scenarios, the worst case scenario will become reality, is really, really small.

> **66** *I am an old man and have known a great many troubles,*
> *but most of them never happened.* **99**
> *Mark Twain*

Just like Mark Twain I have dozens of worst case scenarios in my head. They are about travelling, love, work, relationships, health, money....you name it and I will give you a limiting belief about it. But I have to conclude that none (well, except for one, I will tell you more about it later) has become reality. Most of the time my Unlikeliness Strategy works really well for me to cope with some of the limiting beliefs that pop up in my head.

The second strategy I want to share with you is one I learned from Tim Ferriss. His strategy to deal with his own limiting beliefs is the one I call the "Emergency Plan Strategy". Tim takes his limiting belief and the worst case scenario that goes along with it and lifts it to the next level. He creates an emergency plan, outlining what to do in case the worst case scenario actually becomes reality. This allows him to understand two important things when dealing with limiting beliefs. First of all, he knows that if his worst nightmare becomes a reality, he has a plan ready to clean up the mess. Secondly, it makes him realise that this worst case scenario can be rectified in a much easier way than his limiting belief led him to believe. Looking at his beliefs in this way gives him the confidence needed to cope with them.

A third strategy you can use to deal with your limiting beliefs is described by Tara Mohr in her bestseller 'Playing Big'. She believes that when we take steps to do big things in our lives, we all experience fear. When we start playing big, our limiting beliefs and worst case scenarios pop up like mushrooms in autumn. She offers another great strategy to cope with them. I call her strategy the "I-Do-It-Anyway Strategy". She advises to solely listen to what our limiting belief wants to tell us, but not to act upon it. The aim of her strategy is not to switch off the belief in our head – because that doesn't work anyway – but to recognise it when it's playing, so we can acknowledge its existence without acting upon it.

WHEN YOUR LIMITING BELIEF SHOWS UP AS AN EXCUSE NOT TO GO AFTER YOUR DREAMS.

It is possible that your limiting beliefs will show up in your life disguised as an excuse. I happen to know the two most common excuses which people use for not living the life of their dreams.

The first excuse is money. Or rather the lack of it.

If I got one euro each time I hear "I don't have the money" as the reason why somebody is not living his or her dreams, I would be a millionaire by now. If you are telling me "I don't have the money" I know that it is fear disguised as a perfect excuse to not do anything at all. Not having money is a limiting belief inside your head which presents itself as a fact. And you have chosen to live your life by it. But have you ever realised you actually have money? Of course you have! You were able to buy this book. So please, I would like you to return to the paragraph in this book about how to deal with limiting beliefs and start using any of the three strategies to deal with them. If you have other limiting beliefs going through your mind related to money (like "Nobody is going to pay me to chase my dreams"), please go back to the same paragraph. You have limiting beliefs around money and they have disguised themselves as excuses. They are holding you back to be the most amazing version of yourself. If you want to live the life of your dreams and fulfil your mission, you need to learn how to deal with these limiting beliefs first. You know the strategies by now.

What other stuff do I frequently hear when people tell me that they do not chase their dreams?

They tell me: "I don't have time. With kids and a job and a partner and all those things, I am too busy".

Again, this is fear talking. Fear disguised as the perfect excuse for not doing anything at all. 'Not having time' is a worst case scenario and it is presenting itself as a fact. But of course you have time! You are reading this book, after all. "I do it when the kids have gone to bed", "I do it when I am retired", "I do it when…" It is time for you to face reality! This mission of yours is not going to happen unless you make it happen!

"IT'S NOT GOING TO HAPPEN UNLESS YOU MAKE IT HAPPEN!"

Even if you really believe you don't have time, by cheerfully singing along with your limiting belief, you are wasting your time like a pro. So please, return to the paragraph above about how to deal with this.

Not having money or not having time are two of the limiting beliefs I hear the most. But there are many, many more. When the very first draft of this book was sent to a test panel, the readers shared some thoughts about the content with me. And these thoughts were exactly in line with what I was expecting to hear because I heard them hundreds of times over the years, in different versions and in different places. Their thoughts were similar if not the same as all the feedback I receive when I tell the story of my life. I share some of them here with you, because I am sure that some of these thoughts have gone through your mind as well while reading this book:

- ❖ Yes, interesting story, but my life is far more complicated than yours, Lien!
- ❖ Yes, inspiring, but you don't have a partner/family/kids to take into account.
- ❖ Yes, but not everybody can resign from their jobs that easily! I have bills to pay.
- ❖ Yes, but I don't have an economic background or capital or an entrepreneurial experience like you.

I know that the thoughts mentioned above have gone through your mind too whilst reading this book. And I understand well enough that a so-called lack of money, or time, or knowledge or any other reason works as the perfect excuse for you once life is giving you the option to start fulfilling your dreams. But if you have paid close attention reading this chapter you have already discovered that we all have our limiting beliefs (including me!) and that we can all use different strategies to cope with them:

- ❖ The Unlikeliness Strategy
- ❖ The Emergency Plan Strategy
- ❖ The I-Do-It-Anyway Strategy

If these 3 strategies are not enough, there is a fourth strategy which can help you cope with the limiting beliefs inside your head. You can reformulate your worst case scenario into a question. Instead of endlessly repeating the belief "I don't have money", you can rephrase it into the question "How can I make money while chasing my dreams?" Instead of the dead-end statement "I don't have money", you have reformulated it into a constructive and open question that creates space for action. The same goes for "I don't have time" which you can rephrase into "How can I create time so I can work on my mission?" The good thing about those reformulations is that you can immediately start acting upon the constructive questions that arise.

Despite all the strategies above, I know there are worst case scenarios haunting your head and I am sure you are convinced that your limiting beliefs are true. I am also convinced that your life is a complex construction of many dependencies and that you believe you don't have the right skills, or the necessary knowledge or the right network to make it all work. I believe that you believe all of that is true.

But you know what?

I believed this to be true for myself as well.

More than that: it was the truth back in 2011. I didn't have the necessary knowledge, I didn't have the network, I didn't have enough money and I simply didn't know what I started when I wrote that very first What-I-Want Manifesto. And yet I wrote it and I started acting upon it. I stopped being a cry-baby, wiped away my tears and I did something about it. It may sound harsh to you but nobody is interested in your story as to why you cannot change anything. We all have heard these what-if stories thousands of times and they are not interesting at all. You wouldn't be reading this book either if it would be about how I discover my mission to become an Explorer of Life, only to cite in the next chapter all kinds of excuses for why I don't do anything with this mission.

HOW DOES IT FEEL TO SEE A WORST CASE SCENARIO UNFOLD IN A FOREIGN COUNTRY?

There are people who describe me as adventurous. Whether this is true or not depends on the definition you use. I am not afraid to go on a trip on my own, including to places that are not considered as Standard Travel Destinations. I often end up in these places sleeping in a hut with cockroaches and eating something that most of us would categorise as a pet, but I am not sure if this makes my life adventurous.

But in 2012 I take a trip around the north of Thailand that even I consider adventurous. On a worn-out scooter I am taking a 5 days road trip all by myself. This little adventure is preceded by loads of worst case scenarios going through my mind, each one of them making me doubt my plans (do I really have to?) and expressing my worst fears (I am not going to get robbed, am I?). My brain was saying: "No! No! No!" But as you already know I don't allow myself to be stopped by my panicky worst case scenario thinking brain, nor by a lack of experience or knowledge.

By travelling a lot I have been able to experience that when worst case scenarios actually become a reality, everything turns out just fine. Like little miracles happening. Flat tire with the motorbike? No stress, we will pass a mechanic. No hotel booked? There is always a place to sleep. Ran out of fuel? No worries, somebody is selling a litre of it at the other side of the road. After having lived and survived through such situations one can only conclude that everything always works out fine.

I was so blessed that I already learned this valuable lesson at the moment my face hit the hot Thai asphalt and my scooter comes to a stop. On top of me. After 15 minutes of excruciating pain and crying my eyes out, a fantastic couple (Sakba and Mew) stops and brings me to their home hidden in a gigantic banana plantation in a gorgeous mountain range nearby. There they do what Thai do best: they smile, take care of me, feed me and make sure I am ok. All I can think of is: "You see, even when the worst case scenario hits, everything will always work out fine."

WHAT IF YOUR WORST CASE SCENARIO IS A Y2K: THE POWER OF THE 'BEST CASE SCENARIO'.

Imagine in what kind of world we would live if we all hear our own hit parade of limiting beliefs, only to joyfully continue building our mission anyway. Imagine all the things that would be possible if you would stop doing the things which endlessly annoy you today. Imagine which unique path you would have followed in your life if you hadn't allowed your limiting beliefs to hold you back. Just imagine.

In my hit parade the limiting belief "Travelling forever is a dream" has always been playing. It has been my favourite sing-along-song for most of my life. The lyrics were written many years ago. This song is my instinct that wanted to protect me with the best of intentions against all kinds of disasters and worst case scenarios. Until I began to realise that this song was preventing me from making my dreams come true. By now I know that I can sing along to the song, but that I don't need to act upon it. It's just a stupid song in my head. A stupid, meaningless song.

The liberation I felt when I first heard the limiting belief without listening slavishly to it, was such a delight! A whole new world – literally – opened up to me. Even better, my head exploded! Again! I showed my middle finger and said: "Fuck off, you limiting belief".

The strong belief that I wouldn't be able to travel for the rest of my life had stopped me from doing what I really wanted to do, what I really had to do, what I must do: to be an Explorer of Life.

By mid-2012 I was completely done with using my beliefs as excuses over and over again!

CHAPTER 4

'JUST ACT NORMAL'

WHY IT IS SO HARD TO FOLLOW OUR DREAMS.

By the end of 2012, after my scooter accident in Thailand, I was ready to shout "Fuck off" to some of the most depressing limiting beliefs in my head. At that time I still hadn't got a clue how to become an Explorer of Life or what steps I should take to become one. Although I didn't know what to do, I was hopeful. I had good reasons to be so. Because during my travels I got to know real people who'd been doing what I wanted to do and they had been doing it for years. I now had role models who showed me the possibilities. They might have different limiting beliefs than me to deal with and for sure their path wouldn't be exactly the same as mine, but I knew I could learn from them anyway.

By early 2013 I'd already had a little taste of what it would feel like to finally make my dreams come true and live them. The sweet after-taste of my Asian travels was still lingering in my mouth. I discovered what my dream life would look like in real life. Now that I experienced what living like an Explorer of Life felt like, there was only one question left unanswered: 'How the hell am I going to make this happen in the long run?' Because there are a few practical obstacles standing in the way. I have my flourishing consultancy company which I founded 3 years earlier, with fantastic clients I love working for. I signed some long-term deals with them and I am blessed to be working with clever employees in a beautiful office. I also have two mortgages which are still running for another 20 years or so and I have all my stuff which I'd been collecting over the years. So transitioning from a life whereby I travel for a couple of months a year into a life whereby I live as a nomadic Explorer of Life full time was not going to be quick nor easy. But I decided to walk this path from the moment I discovered my mission and I am not going to turn back.

But although I am determined I am also wondering where on earth I am going to find the courage to make some of the difficult choices and sacrifices needed in the months (and maybe the year) ahead. How much resistance will I have to deal with? How many limiting beliefs from the people around me will I have to break through? How am I going to defend the unconventional choices I am about to make when I am not really sure where this whole mission-chasing-journey will take me?

The only big question left unanswered: "How the hell am I going to make this happen?"

So I still had a couple of things to figure out when I crossed the Vietnam border in the spring of 2013.

LIVING YOUR DREAM EVERY SINGLE DAY IS MUCH MORE DIFFICULT THAN ONE MIGHT THINK.

Do it or not? Jump into that new exciting adventure or better not? Chase that powerful mission you have or not? The stats give a very clear answer. Most people won't. Even if they have the chance to pursue the life of their dreams, they won't. "Most people will choose unhappiness over uncertainty" Tim Ferriss writes in 'The 4-Hour Work Week'. And he is absolutely right! The feelings of uncertainty we experience are often much stronger than the courage we need when we are about to step off the predefined path ahead of us and onto that new, yet unknown path. Our fear of failing is often more powerful than our feeling of restlessness.

The fact that you are reading this book means that deep inside, you want to step away from that restlessness. You feel that the time has come to finally fulfil your life's mission. For quite some time you've felt that you do not have any other option left than to go for it. You don't feel like you can take another compromise. You are going to take the leap and stop fulfilling everyone else's expectations about how you should live your life. You have taken the decision to start walking on the beat of your own drum and that simple fact makes you the exception to the rule. Maybe it took you years to finally find the courage to seek and go after your mission at full speed. But now you will have to maximise your willpower to keep on going. Because the consequence about making that decision to be an exception is that you will have to justify yourself. And from my experience, I know that you will have to justify your choices over and over again. And then a 100 times more.

"HOW THE HELL AM I GOING TO EARN MONEY AND LIVE THE DREAM?"

From that moment back in 2012 when I discovered that my unique mission is to be an Explorer of Life, some small, tiny, little worries popped up into my brain: 'How the hell am I going to make the dream work and how am I going to earn money whilst living it?"

Some days it looked like dozens of practical obstacles were standing in the way between me and my mission. I had to move all my stuff to a store room, I wanted to sell my car, I needed to renegotiate contracts, and so much more. It seemed like a never-ending stream of practical arrangements. But those were by far not my biggest concerns. There was something far more nagging. I imagine it might sound totally crazy to you that there was an obstacle far bigger than selling my houses or restructuring my business. An obstacle that I couldn't ignore...

Where am I going to find the courage to make all those choices that are necessary so I can live my mission and do what I must do in life? And where am I going to find the willpower to keep going for it when things get really messy?

As an entrepreneur I have read hundreds of articles and books about coping with fear and taking risks. Every expert confirms that all risks are less creepy once we've taken them. That's exactly where the Catch-22 is. In order to find out that taking the first step isn't all that scary, you have to actually take that first step. But in order for you to dare to take it, you want to know beforehand that this step is getting you somewhere, because that is how you can reduce the risk. But you really can't know beforehand if a step will lead you to somewhere better. So you end up not taking that first step at all. The result is that you end up going nowhere.

What we often forget when we are considering taking that first step is that when we don't seem to like this new path, we always have the option to simply retrace our footsteps. It is very rare that after just one step we have burned the path we left behind us. Your brain and its limiting beliefs want you to think that you "are throwing it all away". But in almost any circumstance you can pick up your old life again, just where you left it and without all too much trouble. So when you are considering that first step and you have been doing so for days, weeks, months or even years, just know this one thing: That first step, no matter how scary (and exciting) it might seem, is always reversible.

But, oh, irony!

There is a real chance that once you have taken that first step and started taking action towards your mission, you won't feel like retracing your footsteps at all. You've started marching to the beat of your own drum and that beat sounds pretty amazing and exciting. Anyone who has ever quit a job to launch his or her own business will agree: "I never ever want to work for a boss again." Once you've tasted the sweetness of walking your own unique path, it is impossible to return to your bitter past.

THE MOST OVERRATED CHARACTER TRAIT WHEN CHASING YOUR DREAMS: COURAGE.

Courage is like the black box in an airplane to me. It is hard to get the concept, let alone to fully understand it. We say that someone is courageous when this person does something that we don't dare to do ourselves. We all have examples of people we find courageous. For me personally, courage means doing something that you have never done before and of which you are not 100% certain of the outcome. Looking at courage from this viewpoint you understand that we are most courageous when we learn new things, develop new skills or experience new adventures. Because these are the moments in our lives when we don't know in advance whether we will succeed. We do not know beforehand whether we will master that skill or enjoy that new adventure. We don't know if this new skill we learned will end up being useful to us. It might be that we have just been wasting our time, our money or both.

When you look at kids you understand that they are the most courageous of us all. When you have seen kids racing down a ski slope you know what I mean. Kids don't seem to know fear or think about whether they will be able to learn something new. They just try and do. They learn how to cycle without stabilizers, even when they don't know whether they will stay upright or painfully crash on the asphalt. They learn how to talk without knowing how the grammar works and whether they will ever make a correct sentence. If they don't manage to walk at their first attempt after they are done with crawling, they just try again! As a society we strongly stimulate this learning process. We encourage (there is the word 'courage' again) kids to take risks. We know that progress only comes from trying, over and over again. Therefore we help kids to find the courage to keep going and we applaud them at every fresh attempt they make.

And then, at a certain point in life, all this amazing encouragement comes to an end.

Sometime in our teenage years the applause we used to get for taking risks stops. Even worse: the older we get, the more intolerant we become to risks. Risks are no longer considered a necessary part of our growth and development process, but rather become something which needs to be avoided at all cost. Suddenly 'much is at stake' and there is 'a lot to lose'. That's what we tell ourselves and that's what we tell each other. This 'you shouldn't take such big risks' is probably the most persistent limiting belief we tell ourselves in our Western society. So when you go after your dreams, you will not only have to learn how to cope with your own limiting beliefs but also how to cope with all the beliefs of the people around you.

Apart from unlearning how to take risks, something else happens when we grow older. We start to forget the pleasure that comes with trying something for the very first time. We tend to forget the satisfaction we feel when we succeed in something after tens or hundreds of trial and error. Yet nothing is as thrilling as trying something you are a tiny bit afraid of. Afterwards you will usually say: "I am happy I did it." You were nervous and probably a bit scared, but you did it anyway. And that made you feel proud and good about yourself.

> "WE FORGET THE PLEASURE AND THE SATISFACTION THAT COMES WITH TRYING SOMETHING FOR THE FIRST TIME OR SUCCEEDING IN SOMETHING FOR THE FIRST TIME AFTER LOTS OF TRIAL AND ERROR."

Each time you do something of which you don't know what the outcome will be, you need courage. Somewhere deep inside you, you need to find the strength to do this new thing without knowing if it is going to work out or not. Because this strength can only come from deep within our courage is something very personal. What you consider courageous ("I would never dare to do that") is maybe completely normal to someone else. Something which is very normal to you ("That's just normal") will be considered courageous by others.

"DO SOMETHING EVERY DAY THAT SCARES YOU" IS THE WORST ADVICE EVER.

"Do something every day that scares you" the famous quote says. To some daredevils doing something that scares them means freediving into the ocean as deep as 250 meters. To others it might be picking up the phone and cold-call a potential client. Personally I think it's way too exhausting to do something that scares me every day! My first intuitive reaction is to say 'no' to all new things. But I do realise though that this rejecting reaction doesn't allow me to grow any further in life and therefore it doesn't make me happy either. So although doing something that scares me everyday exhausts me, I also know that it is a good thing to say 'yes' more often to unknown experiences. I know that saying yes to scary things trains my 'Muscle of Courage', a muscle which is crucial in fulfilling my mission and living a purposeful life. Each year I experiment with a couple of things I've never done before. After some of these experiments I say "Never again!" like that time I ate that mushy silkworm in Vietnam. Those little insects are really gross (at least when you eat them) and only thinking about it makes me gag. Luckily enough most of my 'Muscle of Courage' training led to fantastic experiences, even when they frightened me (to death) beforehand. In 2015 I learnt a new language and my biggest fear was to sound like a complete idiot and to look like a fool. But even though speaking a new language scares me, I still speak as much Spanish as possible notwithstanding my wrong grammar and conjugations. I won't let myself be stopped by the idea that 'I will look like a fool' or 'I will consider myself being a language misfit'. This year I am also learning a new sport, wave surfing, and I have to confess to you that surfing requires a lot of courage. Not only am I scared of big waves, I also hurt myself multiple times whilst surfing reef breaks and ended up at the doctor's office on a number of occasions. On top of that, the courage one needs to just keep trying over and over again at surfing and still suck at it, is ridiculous. Turns out that surfing is really, really difficult, despite what you might think after seeing movies like Point Break or The Endless Summer. Most times I've come out of the water looking like a nearly drowned dog. I never look like a surf babe who actually knows what she's doing. My hair never looks like that of those bikini surf babes either. And yet, I surf! Because it teaches me how to handle the feeling of not knowing how to do something and still try. It teaches me how to fail and deal with that. And it teaches me to try again, at least one more last wave, and not give up.

This surfing thing might seem like a lot of hard work to you, so you might wonder why I am so persistent at it; why I have not given up yet.

Because surfing really makes me feel awesome. It only requires 5 seconds of actually standing up on my longboard to make me feel elated for the rest of the day. Surfing makes me feel I can take on the world. It makes me feel good about myself. It makes me feel proud too. It is an amazing feeling to be at one with the ocean. But most of all, it feels fantastic when you suddenly realise that you are very slowly getting better, one wave at a time.

So tell me... why would I deny myself all this pleasure and satisfaction, simply because society tells me time and time again that I shouldn't try new things because it is too risky.

> **66Life is either a daring adventure or nothing at all.99**
> Helen Keller

Learning a new language or learning how to surf might not at all be courageous to you. But someone else might be in cold sweat just thinking about it. Our risk tolerance depends on our positive and negative experiences in the past with taking risks. All these experiences create our personal comfort zone. It is from within this unique comfort zone that every one of us takes risks. This zone can be big or small. Its size depends on how much you stretched it throughout your life. Stretching and getting out of this comfort zone is something everybody can train. You too can practice 'being courageous'. The more you are trained to do things of which you don't control the outcome, the more courageous you will become and the more risks you will be able to take. By training that 'Muscle of Courage' of yours, you will discover which feelings these so-called risks invoke inside you, as well as learn how to deal with them. Hence, becoming more courageous is a personal development thing.

Although I believe that every one of us (including me) should learn how to take more risks, my advice also comes with a little note of warning. Do you know that quote "The magic happens outside your comfort zone"? It is only partly true. And it's also kind of dangerous. Because going way out of your comfort zone leads to being more afraid, not less. When you stretch yourself that much out of your comfort zone that you get into a panic attack, you are taking my advice slightly too far. When you panic, you see your fear confirmed and hence you will become risk-averse instead of increasing your appetite for risks.

So doing something which scares you a bit? Absolutely!

Doing something which provokes a panic attack? To avoid at all times!

BUT WHAT IF IT REALLY SCARES THE SH*T OUT OF ME TO REACH FOR MY DREAMS AND LIVE FREELY?

It is quite possible that you are not yet the person who is ready to take that next step and to start to fulfil your mission today. Maybe you realise that it takes far more courage than you have today to take the first step. Don't beat yourself up over it. Today it might well be that you don't feel like the person you would really love to be, but by developing your 'Muscle of Courage' slowly but surely you are already taking the necessary steps to help you reach for your dreams. Only when we completely turn our backs on our path (just like I'd told myself all my life that 'travelling forever was not for me') that is when we also turn our backs on our dreams and our mission.

So look for a small step that you can take today, because realising your mission will start modestly. With a first step. With a small action. An action you must take. Maybe you have already been procrastinating for weeks, months, years, without taking a single step. Yet it's only by taking this one very first step that you start moving. And once you start moving and before you even realise it, you'll be walking your own unique path. Thanks to this one tiny step. This step you will take today. No magic, no cheerleaders, no marching band, no applause. Only you, your mission and that first step.

> **❝Be yourself. Everyone else is taken.❞**
> Oscar Wilde

If you are excited about training your 'Muscle of Courage' but you don't really know how to, I have a simple yet very effective exercise that leads to instant results. You will need your To Do List at hand for this one. So, take that list and have a look at everything that is on there. I bet that there is something on this To Do List for quite some time now. It isn't something that requires a huge amount of time to do. Maybe you can get the job done in less than half an hour, so not having time is not really the best excuse for not getting this thing done. And yet, you haven't done it today. Just like you didn't do it yesterday or the week before. Have you ever thought why you are procrastinating? Let me take a little guess: you haven't done it yet, because somewhere deep inside you feel resistance to do it and you haven't found the courage yet to overcome that resistance. Procrastination is the clearest symptom of a lack of courage. You need this courage because that thing on your To Do List is something of which you can't predict the outcome. Maybe you have to call your mother to talk about that argument you had over lunch and you have no idea yet whether you will be able to resolve the conflict or whether it will get worse. The fact that you don't know the outcome yet makes you a little nervous or scared. So you procrastinate, over and over again. However, situations like this one are invitations to train your 'Muscle of Courage'. Some people think you need to do crazy stuff to get more courage, but it's actually the little challenges we face each day that provide us with the opportunity to become more courageous and to gain more confidence when it comes to taking risks. Just do that tiny little thing that's been on your To Do List for such a long time. I know you will drag your feet as if you've just received your death sentence but afterwards you will be glad you did it. Even if the outcome is not quite what you expected (or nowhere near), the result will always be that you have a more developed 'Muscle of Courage'. And that is what matters most in the end.

WILLPOWER IS A SHAM. MOTIVATION IS THE REAL DEAL.

Everyone who has tried to quit smoking knows it. Willpower or self-discipline is the most overrated character trait of human beings. Although we love to tell ourselves that we've attained our goals thanks to willpower and self-discipline, nothing could be further from the truth. More and more psychologists, like Kelly McGonigal of the University of Stanford, claim that willpower does not even exist. That it is a myth we came to believe in. In 'The Willpower Instinct' she writes: "My students believe that they have a voice in their head which controls their weaknesses. They fear that if they give up this voice, they have no willpower or self-control at all. If you think the key to willpower is being harder on yourself, you are not alone. But you are wrong." The thing we all label as willpower or self-discipline is in fact the ongoing presence of motivation. Our motivation is what helps us to keep going despite setbacks. If we do not have this motivation present, there will be no will to continue whatever it is that we are doing.

A great story about motivation can be read in Andre Agassi's biography Open. Andre has built one of the most successful tennis careers in recent history. Despite crippling back aches he played at top level for more than 20 (twenty!) years. You might say that he has huge willpower. Yet, that is not what it is about. His career was so impressive because day in day out he found the motivation to get out of bed, pick up that tennis racket and hit a couple of thousand forehands. Before having breakfast. As from the age of six. Only a few people know that Agassi actually hated tennis. From the day he was a little toddler and held a tennis racket for the first time to the day he played his last professional match he detested the game from the bottom of his heart. It made him feel miserable for most of his successful long-lasting career. Where did he find his motivation, day after day? How did he keep up his motivation for all those years, even though he hated the game? The answer is striking: fear. Fear is what kept him motivated. This fear was always around in the form of his powerful, domineering father whose life goal was to turn his son Agassi into a champion. Throughout his extensive career Agassi was only driven by the most negative kind of motivation there is: fear. Tennis was the road that was laid out for him since birth and he never found the courage to deviate from this path so he could walk his own. It was only after he met his future wife Steffi Graf and when he retired from tennis that he finally started to fulfil his own beautiful mission.

The Agassi story shows that you can be incredibly successful on the path that has been predefined for you. This path made Andre feel miserable for the first 40 years of his life. At least he can wipe away his tears with the millions of dollar notes in his bank account. But we should never confuse success with the idea that we are walking our own unique path chasing our dreams. Don't be fooled into thinking that "it has to be my mission, because look how good I am at it". If it doesn't make your heart beat a little faster at the end of the day (and at the end of your life, for that matter), then it simply isn't your path.

> "DO NOT CONFUSE SUCCESS WITH THE IDEA THAT YOU ARE WALKING YOUR UNIQUE PATH."

Just like you and Andre, I also did a couple of things in my life —on a far smaller scale than Agassi admittedly — that can be considered a success (I have messed up a lot of things too but that is for my next book). But despite this success I always got bored after a while. I didn't find it all that interesting anymore, it didn't excite me anymore. But if I am totally honest with myself, it wasn't so much my shrinking interest that made me feel bored. There was something else, something far more fundamental. It was not my interest that I lost somewhere along the road to success. It was my motivation which I lost. After a couple of months (or years) the rewards that came with the success (like money, respect, attention...) faded and didn't give me that rush anymore. The motivation coming from all the external rewards slowly disappeared and I didn't find any motivation within myself to carry on. Once the external rewards no longer excited me, I couldn't find any intrinsic motivation to keep on walking that path to success. So I pulled the plug and found another thing to do, until the same pattern repeated itself, often every 3 years. It happened with jobs, relationships, friends and even my own business ventures. I kept on switching and choosing another path hoping that this time around I wouldn't lose my motivation over time. But I always did. And it made me feel like a quitter.

But I was not a quitter. I just didn't know what I truly wanted in life.

Since I've discovered my mission of being an Explorer of Life, the pattern seems to be broken. The ever-returning three-year cycle is a thing of the past. Some inspiring people I have met throughout the years confirm that when you have found your mission in life you will notice that motivation and courage come from your heart. Walking your unique path and living your dreams are not driven by fear (like in Agassi's case) or by extrinsic motives (like money or applause) but only by positive emotions.

The energy which comes from these emotions is crucial in fulfilling my mission as an Explorer of Life. It is the force which drives me and I need a lot of it. And when I write a lot, I mean a loooooooot. Because being an explorer means I have to pack my bags over and over again, find ways to finance my lifestyle time and time again, invest bucket-loads of time in making new friends and in building relationships and I have to say goodbye all the time. All of this can be bloody exhausting. And yet this is what I want. Still. Since 2012. The motivation comes from deep within. From my heart. Not because someone else thinks I should be an Explorer of Life. Not because I am rewarded to do so or because I get applause for it. Not because I can make a nice living with it. No, those are not the real rewards. The reward is in how fast my heart beats at night and how my soul feels during the day. And this every single day of the year. Despite all the obstacles, all the setbacks and all the insecurity, I wouldn't dream of quitting. I wouldn't think of choosing another path. I think I've only recently become fully aware that I might well be on my very own, unique path in life. A path that can only be walked by me.

"I THINK I'VE ONLY JUST BECOME AWARE THAT I MIGHT WELL BE ON MY UNIQUE PATH."

Although motivation is key when you chase your dreams, it is not something you can train like your 'Muscle of Courage'. It's impossible to train yourself to stay motivated. You can somewhat stimulate motivation extrinsically (with money, recognition and status for instance) but this will always run dry and disappear after a while. Maybe that has been the way you have been living your life and maybe you have been wondering why the hell you always felt so exhausted and restless. But remember that you will only find motivation within yourself when you are walking a path which is truly unique to you. When you are fulfilling your mission and you walk your own path, the motivation comes to you like an unlimited source of energy. You become like those Duracell rabbits that keep on going. You can't do otherwise than to just go on and on and on. Not because you are afraid of something, not because you tricked yourself into thinking that there is a reward waiting for you at the other side of the mountain. No. You keep going because you know that this path which you are on right now, is utterly perfect for you.

CHAPTER 5

LIVING THE DREAM!

OH WAIT, IT DOESN'T
HAPPEN THAT FAST!

YOUR DREAM IS LIKE A BORDEAUX: IT NEEDS TIME TO FULLY DEVELOP.

How cool would it be to do that thing you love most and do it every day from morning till night? How would you feel if you could spend all your time on realising your mission? And what if you were making enough money while doing so? I can tell you, it's really awesome! But, I can also tell you that from time to time it's pretty damn hard too. Having the courage to choose your own path is one thing, but making a living out of it year after year is something totally different.

> **66Some men see things as they are and say why.
> I dream things that never were and say why not.99**
> G.B. Shaw

For those of you who have walked those first steps on your own unique path, however tiny those steps might be: this chapter is for you. It will help you to find the motivation to continue doing what you love. I will help you to overcome the obstacles that are guaranteed to cross your path towards your dream life. A life where you fulfil your mission without worrying about money issues.

But how do you get started practically? Because right now you might well have a job which has nothing to do with your mission and which simply serves to pay the bills. Or maybe you are already busy realising your mission, but the money is not following. Or maybe you make tons of money with your mission-driven company, but you feel like it owns you.

No matter where you are at in the realisation of your mission, there are certain things you need to do and others you need to let go. Have a look at these five different phases and identify which one applies most to you right now:

- The first phase of living your dream life (also called The Rat Race Phase): you have a job to pay the bills and it takes so much of your time that you have almost no time to work on your dream (sometimes you can spend a day, then you don't work on it for another 6 days, then you have a couple of hours the week after, etc.). Chasing your dream seems totally impossible at this point of your life.
- The second phase of living your dream life: you invest as little time as necessary in a job (maybe you are working part-time) which just brings some money into your bank account. But you don't make any money with your mission yet.
- The third phase of living your dream life: you are making money with your mission but it's just about enough or just about not (depending on the month) to get by.
- The fourth phase of living your dream life (also called The 5% Club): you have built a company around your mission and you make enough money doing so. Yet, you have become some kind of a slave of your dream company.
- The ultimate phase of living your dream: you make more money than you can spend with the fulfilment of your mission and you can dedicate all the time you want on it (whether that is a little or a lot). You are living the dream!

HOW CLOSE ARE YOU TO LIVING YOUR DREAM LIFE?

Which phase are you currently in? Are you already in the ultimate phase or are you still quite far away?

WHICH PHASE ARE YOU I

Regardless of the phase you are currently in, you need to understand one important thing. It is something most people don't want to hear when I mention it. But it is the truth and I prefer to tell you now: moving through those 5 phases is like an elimination race: most of us – maybe you too – have anchored ourselves in the first phase. You have a job and no time at all to chase your dream. This phase is definitely the hardest to get out of and many of us will never succeed. A massive elimination takes place when you move from the first phase to the next. You will notice that most people around you won't follow you. Your tribe will get thinner and thinner when you keep on moving through the phases. Only very few people on earth succeed in achieving the ultimate phase where they can shout out loud "I'm living the dream and it's f*cking amazing!"

> **66Don't ask what the world needs.**
> **Ask what makes you come alive.**
> **And go do that.**
> **Because what the world needs is**
> **people who come alive!99**
> *Howard Thurman*

Apart from understanding that these five phases form an elimination race, there is another thing you need to know about living the life of your dreams. Although I am using the word 'race' it is actually not a race at all, nor is it a sprint. If you are hoping for quick and instant success you need to know that it is very, very unlikely to happen to you or to anyone else. If you expect to fulfil your mission and live your dreams as of tomorrow and on top of that make huge amounts of money in doing so, you are in for a big disappointment. As with all good things, this shit takes time! To pass from one phase to another you will have to make choices which are not easy and therefore require time. Time to think, time to evaluate, time to build confidence, etc. Sometimes that means an awful lot of time. So moving towards your dream life is not a race but a lifelong process. Take it slow and make sure you enjoy the ride itself.

"AS WITH ALL GOOD THINGS, THIS SHIT TAKES TIME!"

In case you are wondering now whether you will ever reach the last phase... I can confirm that it is absolutely possible! In case you are wondering how, my answer is very straightforward: you need to take that first scary step. Every day thousands of people take that first step; away from that predefined road in front of them and straight onto their own unique path. Every dream starts with this first step, followed by a second one. And gradually you are walking from one phase to another.

On the next couple of pages I describe in more detail the first four phases we all walk through when we start living the life of our dreams. I suggest you immediately turn to those pages describing the phase you are currently in. In doing this, you´ll immediately find out which next steps you can take.

I CAN DO WHATEVER I WANT
I CAN DO WHATEVER I WANT
I CAN DO WHATEVER I WANT
I CAN DO WHATEVER I WANT
I CAN DO WHATEVER I WANT
I CAN DO WHATEVER I WANT
I CAN DO WHATEVER I WANT
I CAN DO WHATEVER I WANT

THE MOST DIFFICULT PHASE TO BE IN:

YOUR JOB IS TAKING UP SO MUCH OF YOUR TIME THAT YOU DON'T HAVE ANY TIME LEFT TO WORK ON YOUR MISSION.

Time. Nowadays it has become much more valuable than money. Those who have time in this day and age are the new rich. Having time enables you to get the kids from school and have a chat with the teacher. Having time allows you to curl up on the couch with a book and completely lose yourself in the unfolding story. Having time lets you gaze at the stars at night. When you have time you can go out for dinner with your partner on a weekday, chat for hours and really listen to each other, just like you used to.

If there's anything that we long for more than money, it's time.

"I want to do what I love most every day, and that is making jewellery. But with my busy job and 2 little munchkins at home I have no time for this at all!"

It is more likely that time (or the lack of it) will hold you back from realising your dreams than money. If you are in the phase where you have no (or hardly any) time to fulfil your mission, then you are in the most difficult phase of all. This phase is that so-called rat race we all try to escape from and to our collective frustration we are not very successful at it. Those who succeed in leaving this Rat Race Phase behind them have taken the hardest and most important step towards realising their dream life. But in case you are still in this phase, how do you make that first step?

START BY EXCHANGING YOUR MONEY FOR MORE FREE TIME.

What is the best thing to do when you are stuck in The Rat Race Phase? Actually, it's really simple. In order to be able to go to the next phase you need to start working fewer hours. How do you work fewer hours? Again, very simple and you have a couple of options to choose from:

- ❖ Quit. Your. Job! Stop spending time on a job which eats all your time (not to mention your soul) and for which you only receive a handful of money in return. Quit it!
- ❖ Quitting is not an option? Then work fewer hours. Start working part-time or take a temporary break from it. If your job does not bring you closer to the fulfilment of your mission, then reduce the time you spend on it as much as possible. If the boss says no to your request to work part-time, it could be a gift from heaven (and then it is time to quit anyway).
- ❖ If you are your own boss with your own company but you are doing something that doesn't make your heart beat a little faster, reduce the time you spend working on your company. You are your own boss, so you need to be serious about your own request to work part-time.

This first Rat Race Phase is the hardest to get out of and your main focus should be on creating more time to work on your mission. You – and only you! – are the one who can make sure that you start working fewer hours in that job which doesn't make you feel fulfilled. Your goal should be to have at least 4 out of 7 days available to work on your mission.

Before you start shouting "Yes but I need that money, I have bills to pay. I can't just quit my job!" keep calm and read on.

SO YOU HAVE A JOB BUT NO MONEY, YOU SAY? IT'S TIME TO CONQUER THOSE LIMITING BELIEFS IN YOUR HEAD.

Nobody has money. Or at least so it seems. Because that's what most of us say, all the time. We never seem to have enough of it, however much money we actually possess. I know that we all need a certain amount of money to finance a certain lifestyle. Those bills need to be paid and unfortunately you can't pay them with potato peels.

Now don't get me wrong. I am not saying you don't need that money you currently earn doing whatever job you do right now. I am also not saying that money is an evil thing which needs to be avoided at all costs. I love money! It is the fuel of the society we all live in. Yet it has some massive downsides that keep us trapped. One of them being what I call 'the postponed life': I am going to work hard now, try to save as much money as possible and once I am retired I will finally do all those things which I really love doing. The postponed life is exactly what I was living back in 2011. Working my ass off, saving money and in the meantime dreaming of my early retirement. But the postponed life is a devious illusion which leads to many dreams being taking into the grave. When you have a look at your life with a long term perspective, devious illusions are not what you want to see. You need to get clear and upfront about your life and what it is that makes it all worthwhile. Now is the time to do that. So do what you must do. Now. Not later. Because later might never come. And even if it does come you will probably not be at your best creatively, physically or mentally speaking.

> "SO DO WHAT YOU MUST DO. NOW. NOT LATER."

Saying all that, I do understand that you want a financial buffer. As you are now starting to exchange your money for more free time, a buffer gives you a sense of security to (dare to) go for it. This buffer can be some savings you have on your bank account, or a small loan from friends, family or the bank, or maybe your life partner who can offer you temporary financial support... Any of these help to bridge the gap in which you will have less or no income. A financial buffer makes it easier to escape from this difficult Rat Race Phase you are currently in. So how much buffer should you foresee? Most entrepreneurs advise to have a financial buffer of about three months of expenditure. Enough time to experiment with your dream life, but not too much to make you lazy. Although a financial buffer of three months is not insurmountable, it certainly was for me back in the days. When I decided to run as hard and as far as I could from the Rat Race Phase back in 2010 I had no financial buffer. Nothing. And by nothing, I mean absolutely nothing. I even had to borrow money from my mother to simply register my company. This created a situation where there was no way back. I had to go for it right away. There was no Plan B, no safety net, no buffer. I sometimes think that it worked out well for me, simply because I had no other option. Saying that, I would always advise to do what you feel comfortable with. Just don't allow the limiting belief of 'not having the money' to be a showstopper for you.

> **I hope you live a life you're proud of.**
> **If you find that you are not,**
> **I hope you have the strength to**
> **start all over again.**
> *F.S. Fitzgerald*

So, just to summarize, your first focus when you are in the Rat Race Phase is 'time' and how to create more of it (or at least create enough time for you to be able to work on your dream). In the short term this will very likely lead to a reduction of your personal income. It might even drop to zero. Because moving from the phase you are in and into the next one, you'll have to temporarily give up money to get more time; essential time to develop your mission further and to research if you can earn a living with it. You need to be willing to face this loss of income and just deal with it. At least for now, being at the beginning of your journey.

THE SECOND PHASE:

YOU DON'T MAKE MONEY WITH YOUR MISSION, BUT YOU HAVE PLENTY OF TIME TO WORK ON IT.

When you have identified yourself being in the second phase you have taken the hardest step in realising your mission: you have given up the easy money you got from your job and exchanged it for plenty of time. Phew, you have come this far. You should be proud of yourself. Because most people never make it to this phase. At least not before they retire. Remember I told you this was an elimination race? Well, you have taken the first big hurdle. You have now created time. And time is worth an awful lot.

What you shouldn't do now is get too comfortable in this situation. Don't enjoy all this free time by lounging on the sofa and do nothing with this present you have given yourself. I don't want you to end up as a poor person with a mission. However romantic the image of the poor but creative artist might be, nothing is less romantic than opening your mailbox every day with a pounding heart, scared of receiving another bill you can't pay. I have been there and it is awful. In this second phase you should spend every free hour you have created to do these two things:

- ❖ Work on your mission! Fully and unconditionally. Experience the feeling this gives you. Feel the energy, the drive and the joy that breezes in through the windows and doors of your life. This is a fantastic phase to be in, so enjoy those unprecedented vibes of energy and flow. Enjoy and don't stress. Don't stress.
- ❖ Explore how your mission can help you to pay your bills in the short run and mid-term. Just remember how amazing it would be if you can actually live off this mission in the future? How cool would it be to pay your bills with painting, coaching, surfing, or whatever your true mission is?

HOW CAN I PAY MY BILLS WITH MY MISSION?

The good news is that there is not one, but two ways how to pay your bills with your mission. Both are fairly simple, although they might not look like it at first.

The first option is to look for a job in which it is possible to spend your on-the-job-time working on your mission. Unfortunately the chance that you will actually find this kind of a job is very limited. Most jobs are not created to do whatever you want on your terms. More likely, your own unique path probably doesn't follow the same direction as the company's. You'll need to follow the company's rules and they might not be in line with your mission. Companies want to straightjacket you into a job with a fixed job description, responsibilities and deadlines. Maybe you might still be happy to water your wine for now. But the longer you walk your own unique path, the less you will be prepared to do so.

The other option to pay your bills with your mission is to become your own boss. I believe this option is currently the only real choice we've got left in our Western society if you want to allow your mission to fully flourish, unconditionally and on your own terms. I have been my own boss since 2010 and having my own company has shown to be key to create my dream life. The limits of someone else's company would never have helped me to succeed and live my life to the fullest.

TURNING A MISSION INTO A COMPANY, IS THAT EVEN POSSIBLE!?

Starting a company around what you love sounds great, doesn't it? Building a company based on your mission offers a lot of advantages: it gives you all the necessary energy to keep going when things get hard (and they will!). On top of that you often already have a huge amount of knowledge about your mission which will benefit you once you get started.

When you are considering building a company around your mission, you´ll first have to be aware that you cannot turn every single one of your passions into something people want to actually buy. If you look at those who succeed in turning their mission into a company you will discover that they know very well that they don't get paid for their passion, but they get paid for the products and services they have developed around it. To give an example: it goes without saying that as an Explorer of Life I am passionate about travelling and I love blogging about it. Even though a lot of people read that blog (as a dreamy pastime on a cold Monday morning over coffee in their boring office, I imagine) this blog is not a potential company. First of all, this blog is way too small for most advertisers to be interested. Secondly, if I want to turn this blog into a company I will have to offer products or services which are interesting to my readers: a unique travel guide packed with tips on how to travel solo as a woman or an inspiring adventure trip they can join. This way I am turning my mission as an Explorer of Life into a product or a service for which someone might be willing to pay. If you find a way to offer something (a custom-made motorbike, a unique travel guide, a handmade piece of jewellery, ...), you can definitely make money by fulfilling your mission.

Besides turning your mission into a physical product you also have the option to generate income by teaching or coaching others so they can learn the skills that you already master. In our Western society we are constantly busy with personal development in all kinds of ways and we are willing to pay for it. A lot. Is it your big mission to restore old-timer cars and bring them back to life? Then you can either refurbish someone's old-timer and get money doing that. Or you can teach other old-timer lovers the skills that are necessary to restore their own cars themselves.

For those like me who have a less tangible mission, the search for a commercial application is less straightforward. My mission and my very reason for being here on this planet is to be an Explorer of Life. Although that might sound really cool, it raises the question 'how the hell do I make money with it?' Can I turn my life as an Explorer of Life into a sellable product or a service that my clients are looking for? Maybe. I can pass on my knowledge about basically anything by turning it into products and ask money for these. The paying content on my website about starting and building a small company illustrates this. This book too is a product through which I can share and sell my expertise as an Explorer. Besides creating and selling products like online articles and books, I can also transform my knowledge into a service. I could offer personalised mentoring to everyone who wants to live as a digital nomad for example.

There are plenty of opportunities to turn your mission into a money-making machine and the first step is to derive a product or a service from your mission.

EVEN IF I COULD, IS IT A GOOD IDEA TO BUILD A COMPANY AROUND A PASSION?

It's likely that you too can use your mission to generate an income simply by turning it into a product or a service. But is it a good idea to make money with that passion? This might be a strange question to ask as this chapter is all about turning a mission into a money-making machine. But it's not because you can turn a passion into a company that you should. It might not be a wise thing to do. I don't mean from a business point of view. I mean from a personal point of view. Do you want to turn your passion into a job, even if this is a job on your own terms?

With the example I gave before about my travel blog, my honest answer to this question would be "no". Because I know that I hate writing under pressure. And that would be one of the things I ought to do when I make money by writing travel articles. Because I cherish the freedom to write whenever I feel inspired, I just cannot do it because someone wants me to. Travelling and writing about it would become a duty and I do not want to associate travelling with duties. So if you suspect that fulfilling your mission in the long run would become an unpleasant task then it might be better not to do it at all and think about other money-making paths you can explore with your mission.

Before you turn your mission into a 'job' I advise you to answer a few crucial questions:

- ❖ Do you enjoy teaching or sharing your mission with other people?
- ❖ If your mission implies doing a lot of paperwork, would you still like it?
- ❖ Would you like to work for 40 hours a week or much more on it?
- ❖ Have others ever asked you for help related to your mission?

If the answer to all of the questions above is 'Yes', then it's a good idea to consider turning your mission into a company. Because your mission is only a smaller part of the bigger picture called 'a company'.

WHERE 95% OF US GET STUCK: YOU MAKE MONEY BY LIVING YOUR DREAM, BUT YOU'RE ONLY JUST ABOUT ABLE TO FINANCIALLY SURVIVE (OR NOT).

The idea that exceptional creativity and unconditional passion can only come from some kind of miserable situation, is one of the biggest myths ever. I really wouldn't be able to write this book in a dark and humid cellar without windows whilst I am craving for wine and chocolate. Trust me on this one! So when you have embarked on your journey towards more meaning for a little while now, it is my biggest wish for you that you make more than enough money with it.

But I am guessing that by now you`ve already had to drop some really nice things in your life wandering through this third phase. I call this phase The 95% Phase because most people don't make it beyond and get stuck here forever. I know that when you have been in this phase for a while you don't want to sacrifice those really nice things in life much longer! And you shouldn't, just in case you were wondering. In this 95% Phase the time has come to reverse that exchange you did to get out of the first phase. Back then you exchanged your money for more free time so you could get out of that Rat Race Phase. Now is the time to re-exchange and turn your valuable time into some awesome money. Because I know that you desperately need that money to keep going. You need it to keep on walking your unique path. You need that money so that everyone can continue enjoying this mission you are currently sharing with all of us.

The good news is that in this third phase you no longer have to organise this exchange of 'time for money' on the terms of that company you worked for. Now you can do the exchange on your own terms and in order for you to do that in a smart way, you should understand 3 important concepts: know how much money is 'enough', be clear that there is a difference between 'Necessary Money' and 'Fun Money' and understand how you can generate both of them.

THE DIFFERENCE BETWEEN 'NECESSARY MONEY' AND 'FUN MONEY'.

How much money do you need to have enough? That is the first question to ask yourself. The answer will be different for all of us, so I can't give you a fixed number of what 'enough' means. But what I do know is that we all have a dividing line between two types of money. I call these two types 'Necessary Money' on the one hand and 'Fun Money' on the other hand. Necessary Money is the money you need for the basics in your life: a roof above your head, food, safety, education, health. The amount of money you need to fulfil these basics will be different from other people around you. It depends on where you live, on the people who financially depend on you and so on. But, just like me and everybody else, you'll need a monthly amount of money to provide the basics. That amount is your Necessary Money. Anything on top of this is 'Fun Money'. Fun Money is the money you use to go on holidays, to go out for dinner, to put in a savings account for later, to buy a nice car or that slightly too expensive jacket.

ADD "HOW CAN I MAKE FUN MONEY WITH MY MISSION?" TO YOUR VOCABULARY.

Before you start making lots of Fun Money by fulfilling your mission, you need to ensure that you know how to make enough Necessary Money first. I will bring you back to the design board of what a company should do. It is time that you turn your mission into a real company which enables you to pay your bills. When I say 'real company' I don't mean the legal structure of it, but I mean the ins and outs of your company. How is it structured? What do you create or produce or deliver that makes you earn at least all the Necessary Money you need and eventually also make all that Fun Money you love?

When you are answering the above questions you have started making what might well be your very first business model. A business model simply tells you how you will make your Necessary Money and also your Fun Money. Since a few years I use a simple yet complete tool for creating this level of understanding about the businesses I wish to build around my mission of being an Explorer of Life. This tool is called the Business Model Canvas and it has been designed by a guy called Professor Osterwalder. Every single one of my companies is designed on a piece of paper using this canvas and I update it every six months. When you are in the third phase right now and you make just about enough Necessary Money to get by, I advise you to start using the Business Model Canvas right now to analyse what works and what doesn't and take necessary action where needed.

IF YOU KEEP EXCHANGING YOUR TIME FOR MONEY ACCORDING TO THE EXISTING NORMS, YOU ARE SCREWED.

One of the things the Business Model Canvas will clarify for you is at which rate you are exchanging your time for money. Time and money are the two most valuable things we own and we can use them to negotiate. If you have read the previous chapters you know that those who are in the first phase of working on their mission first need to create more time to work on their mission. In order to do so, they will need to quit their job or start working part-time to create that free time they so desperately need. In exchange for this newly gained free time, they will temporarily make less money. This is the exchange they need to make: exchange money (earn less) for time (to get more free time).

For everyone having a job the ratio 'money for time' is well defined by an employment contract. Only every once in a while this ratio can get renegotiated. To give you an idea how the 'money for time' ratio works, here are a few examples. You might want to change euros for dollars or any other currency and maybe the values and the applying employment laws are different depending on the country you live in, but the examples stand in comparison to one another. Let's have a look:

❖ Maybe you work 40 hours/week and (supposing that you work 4 weeks per month) you end up working 160 (40x 4)

hours each month. In exchange for these 160 hours you might get about 1,600 euro/month on your bank account. In this example your money/time ratio is 10 (=1,600 euro/160 hours). Your time (your hour) is worth 10 euro.

❖ Or maybe you work 38 hours and get 2,300 euro in exchange from your boss. Then your hour is worth 15.13 euro (the calculation is 2,300 euro/(38 x4)). Although having a salary of 2,300 euro seems like a big difference to having one of 1,600 euro, your time (your hour) is only worth a meagre 5 euro extra.

❖ To give you a last example: maybe you work 25 hours and get 950 euro in exchange for it. In this case your hour is worth 9.5 euro (=950/(25 x4)).

Whatever your ratio as an employee is, overall there are no crazy differences in the money/time ratios for most employees. In any of the above examples your time as an employee is worth between 9.5 euro and 15 euro. With this money you earned, you can hopefully pay the bills, do something nice from time to time and maybe save some money for later. Every year during the evaluation period you can ask your boss for a pay raise and maybe you even get a few percentages extra. But this increase won't make much difference. So those who keep on selling their time by being someone's employee or by using the same rates as an entrepreneur, will always find it difficult to create the space required (in terms of time as well as money) to make a decent living with fulfilling their mission. Therefore I believe that as long as you are stuck in selling your time for money according to the existing norms, it will not be possible for you to realise your mission in a sustainable way.

So, stop behaving like an employee. Start acting like an entrepreneur.

When you are your own boss you have the freedom to change your euro/hour rate dramatically. I am not talking about changing your rate from 10 to 11 euro per hour. I am talking about changing your rate from 10 to a 100 or even 1,000 euro per hour. Being your own boss enables you to change your euro/hour rate in such a way that it creates all the freedom you need to fulfil your mission and live the life of your dreams. As an entrepreneur you have control over and influence on your euro/hour rate. Most new entrepreneurs don't really understand this concept and therefore struggle financially.

Now hold it!

Before you start thinking that entrepreneurs are all millionaires with a crazy euro/hour ratio you need to be aware that in my home country of Belgium 1 out of 8 self-employed workers lives below the poverty line. I am not sure about the numbers in your country, but I would advise you to have a look at them. Entrepreneurship is not the fastest highway to easy wealth. But it sure is the most accessible instrument to impact your euro/hour ratio. Being able to change this ratio is the key to success and is the way for you to take the next step in your quest for a life full of passion, purpose and fulfilment. So when you are in the third phase making just enough money to get by, maybe still combining that shitty day job with your dream business in the weekends, you need to make that leap. If you want to move into that next phase it is time to go all-in on your entrepreneurship and your mission.

A NOTE ON NECESSARY AND FUN MONEY.

There are parts of your life when 'Fun Money' flows as if it is coming from a never-ending source and there are other times in your life when 'Fun Money' is a totally inaccessible dream. Money flows just like energy. Sometimes there is plenty of it, sometimes there is none of it. Having money and specifically Fun Money makes your life, well yeah, fun. But as you probably already know 'Fun' does not equal 'Happy'. Having Fun Money won't make you happy. You might get that instant rush when spending Fun Money because you can enjoy the moment. But it won't feed your soul. Any kind of money won't make the empty, meaningless feeling disappear when you are not fulfilling your mission during your time on earth. Maybe you are currently spending piles of Fun Money (just like I did back in 2010) trying to ignore and suppress the nagging feeling that keeps on popping up. Those questions that keep on coming back time after time: "But are you really happy?" Money can and will never fill that void.

So when you keep on choosing to spend your time and money on things which are actually meaningless to you and do not help you to share your life's purpose with the world you should seriously consider what is holding you back right now. You have come this far, so what is keeping you small? Which limiting beliefs are going through your mind and are stopping you?

Are you scared of ending up broke? Does it make you feel uncomfortable just thinking about not being able to buy those beautiful things? Are you scared you might 'lose it all'? Is it all too risky?

Just know that the amount of Fun Money you have available to you right now is not related to your willingness to take risks. You might have lots of money in the bank and think 'I don't want to lose it' or you might have nothing in the bank and think 'I can't do it without a buffer'.

> "WHATEVER YOUR SITUATION IS, MONEY CAN ALWAYS BE THE REASON NOT TO DO SOMETHING. JUST AS IT CAN ALWAYS BE THE REASON TO ACTUALLY DO SOMETHING."

In 2010 I founded my first business and I did it at a time when I finally started to make Fun Money as an employee. It was such an amazing feeling that I was finally getting into a more comfortable financial position after years of hard work. You will probably understand that this didn't make it easier to leave my job and become my own boss. I realised that I would have to give up all this Fun Money again. And the Necessary Money too. On top of giving up on something I finally achieved, I didn't know how long I would have to give it up for. Every employee who finds himself or herself in a golden cage knows what I am talking about. Nobody likes losing something they already have. If the feeling of losing is too uncomfortable to you, maybe becoming your own boss and fulfilling your mission is not within your reach yet. I would suggest to start working on dealing with the limiting beliefs inside your head first. Because whatever your situation is, money can always be the reason not to do something. Just as it can always be the reason to actually do something.

THE 5% CLUB:

YOU HAVE A SUCCESSFUL COMPANY THAT FULFILLS YOUR MISSION. BUT YOU ARE A SLAVE TO IT.

When you have used your company to increase your euro/hour ratio you will reach that point at which you have raised it to a level where there is not only plenty of Necessary Money, but also a lot of Fun Money. You have moved from the third phase - where you were just making enough money to get by - into the fourth phase: welcome to The 5% Club. A fantastic achievement and I hope you feel proud about what you have accomplished so far. Not only did you discover your own unique mission in life, you also chose to start building your life around it and now you have come to a point where you also make lots of money with it. I bet your bank account looks like a phone number by now. I have been in this phase too. And although everyone is applauding and you feel pretty good about coming this far I also know there is a flipside.

I bet that you are probably working a lot more hours then you used to when you were an employee. And those hours are not necessarily spent on your mission either. I know from experience that there is a big chance that you are investing a huge amount of time in keeping that company you built around your mission going. Because I know that you don't just simply change your euro/hour ratio from 10 to 100, 500 or even 1000. It doesn't happen 'just like that'. You have to live up to this ratio and your company needs to be able to support it. For those who are in this fourth phase, The 5% Club, and have become a slave of a successful mission company, I advise four steps you can take right now to streamline your business and make your life as an entrepreneur much easier: Eliminate, Bulk, Automate and Outsource. In that order.

DON'T LET YOUR EGO GET IN THE WAY OF FULFILLING YOUR MISSION.

You might not like to hear this but our ego is what prevents many of us from starting to eliminate, bulk, automate or outsource some of our tasks as entrepreneurs. I admit that my ego also bothers me from time to time. Okay, maybe more often than that, I admit. But in order not to remain a slave of my own mission company I had to stop thinking that all those tasks I completed were necessary and could only be done by me, myself and I. That idea is nonsense. I have to admit that lots of my tasks can be done faster by a computer or better by someone else. I can be replaced much more easily than I like to believe. That knowledge hurts my ego at times. But I don't allow this to be an obstacle to further success. I know that those who really want to live a dream life and have a company to fully support that, will have to keep their ego in check. And so do you.

> **Instead of wondering when your next vacation is, you ought to set up a life you don't need to escape from.**
> *Seth Godin*

When you are thinking about all the tasks that potentially can be eliminated, you naturally don't want to eliminate those you actually love to do and which are totally and directly in line with your mission. They are the reason why you have founded your company in the first place, so you want to keep doing those. If your mission is to make the world a better place by painting unique pieces of street art (or being an Explorer of Life like me), you also know by now that making a great living from this requires you to be an accountant, a marketing executive, a lawyer and maybe even an employer. Although painting (or being an Explorer of Life) is your mission, all those other side tasks are required to keep the show going. The mantra Eliminate, Bulk, Automate and Outsource should only be applied to those tasks which keep you from doing what you really want and must do in your life: painting (or exploring in my case). The bigger your company is, the more likely it is that you do a

shitload of tasks that have nothing to do with fulfilling your mission.

"In life you have to do certain things you dislike, that is part of life." my mum often says. But I full-heartedly disagree with her on this one. I believe you can live a life where you spend all your time just doing the things you love. I have experienced that you really don't have to be a millionaire to live like one. The fourth phase is the place to start building your millionaire lifestyle. You know by now I am not talking about the cars and the private jets. I am talking about living a great life, fully in line with your mission and making lots of Fun Money whilst doing it. So when you are in The 5% Club right now, slaving away at your mission company you need to start Eliminating, Bulking and Automating to help you on the way. The ultimate and final step to free yourself from the entrepreneurial shackles you have created is outsourcing.

"YOU REALLY DON'T HAVE TO BE A MILLIONAIRE TO BE LIVING LIKE ONE."

In my case, as an Explorer of Life and the owner of multiple companies, there are a lot of business tasks to which I apply the abovementioned mantra of Eliminate, Bulk, Automate and Outsource. I apply these four steps to all the tasks I don't like doing. For example, I hate all administrative work. I suspect even most of the administrative workers hate it. Who likes shuffling paper (or the digital equivalent) around from left to right all day long?! If you look carefully at how much time you, as a mission entrepreneur, spend on administrative duties, it will make your stomach turn! All admin work leaves me feeling bored: opening and dealing with mail, doing the accounting each month, answering e-mails, doing bank transactions, making presentations, creating invoices, posting messages on social media, writing newsletters and so on. The admin work in a company is endless and if you are in the fourth phase I advise you to apply the mantra Eliminate, Bulk, Automate and Outsource as much as possible. For this, your administrative work is a good place to start.

BULKING OR 'SINGLETASKING' IS THE BEST PRODUCTIVITY HACK EVER.

The past decade were the years of multitasking: checking your mails while posting something on Facebook and in the meantime keeping an eye on your timesheets. In theory it sounds really good but science has proven that 94% of the people don't have the brain to efficiently multitask. The time it takes to switch on your brain to get a certain task done and then switch to another task is simply too long. Moreover, this constant switching has a negative impact on our efficiency. I wish I could multitask in a productive way, but if I am honest with myself, I know I am part of this group of people who can't do it effectively. Of course sometimes I love to be really busy-busy-busy with lots of things going on at the same time. But that has got nothing to do with productivity.

Singletasking is far more efficient than multitasking and the best productivity hack I discovered in the last few years. This became crystal clear to me when I started bulking all of my knowledge tasks, like answering e-mails or creating invoices. I started executing each task in bulk and executed them all at the same time. In the beginning it was a bit of a quest to find a system that worked for me, but now I have 1 day every four weeks during which I respond to all my emails, create my social media posts and do a couple of more tasks I cannot eliminate or automate or wish to outsource just yet. It is by bulking a lot of my work that I realised how fast I could finish these knowledge tasks, just by executing them all at a set time every month.

Not that long ago, I had an interesting discussion with an entrepreneur about singletasking and bulking. I told her about the concept of singletasking and mentioned that I write all my newsletters on one day each month and publish them in an automated calendar for that month. She told me she couldn't do that. She didn't feel able to write all the newsletters for one month all at once. The reason why was that it seemed very boring to her to dedicate herself to this one task and then to repeat this four times (she sends out four newsletter in one month). I told her that I write eight newsletters at a time and indeed creating them all at once is not the most inspiring activity. But getting inspired is not the reason why I bulk this task. The point is that I have finished all tasks related to newsletters in two hours of time for the rest of the month and that this allows me to go surfing on the other 29 days of the month. I don't have to get behind my laptop every week and think about sending yet another newsletter.

The power of bulking your tasks is twofold: it is in creating a habit by repeating the same tasks a couple of times in a row (like writing not one but multiple newsletters or not answering a day's worth of emails but a month's worth) and it is in achieving amazing efficiency gains by means of focus. So the reward of bulking lies in the freedom and flexibility you gain.

FIRST LEARN HOW TO BULK PROPERLY. AUTOMATING AND OUTSOURCING WILL FOLLOW.

Besides the fact that you can finish your knowledge tasks a lot faster, bulking has another important advantage. Once you start bulking your repetitive tasks, you begin to discover their executing patterns. These patterns hidden in all repetitive tasks are impossible to recognise if you don't do these tasks at least ten times in a row. When bulking, you repeat the same task multiple times and you discover patterns in the execution of the tasks. Discovering these patterns is the necessary first step to automate or outsource more of your tasks.

LET SOFTWARE OR SOMEONE ELSE DO THE JOB FOR YOU!

I am not ashamed to tell you I haven't cleaned my house for ages. Actually I am really proud of that. Some people love cleaning but I hate it passionately. This also goes for doing the laundry, the ironing, the gardening, etc. For years now I have outsourced all my housekeeping tasks and I prefer to keep it that way until the day I die.

Many people find it difficult to outsource tasks to a computer or to another human being. I have always wondered why... So I started asking and there appears to be a variety of quite interesting reasons why most people don't want to outsource some of their work. Not being able to give up control is often the most important one. 'When you do it yourself it gets done better'. It seems that mainly women have a hard time with letting go of this idea. But hey, ladies, this doesn't do us any favours! Let it go. A second reason for not outsourcing work is a kind of displaced shame like 'you don't ask someone else to do something if you can do it yourself'. A third reason is that we believe that doing tasks we don't like are 'part of life'.

Whatever reason you come up with in your head to justify why you can't or won't outsource work, let it go. If the popular but limiting belief 'I don't have money for that' goes through your mind right now, I advise you to look at some of the numbers when you think about outsourcing work. When you outsource an hour of housekeeping duties to a cleaning lady who charges 25 euro per hour and in that same hour you could invoice 100 euro to a client, why the hell would you scrub the bathroom floor?

In Belgium we are familiar with outsourcing housekeeping duties. But I learned that it is just as easy to outsource tasks in my company. For years I had a Virtual Assistant who handled all my paper mail (when I still had paper mail. I eliminated it back in 2013), planned a big part of my appointments and did my accountancy work, amongst many other tasks. Besides outsourcing work to her, I also had an assistant in Pakistan who answered all requests for proposals, booked appointments and organised all deposits related to these. At the peak of my business my Pakistani assistant easily saved me 2 to 3 days of work per week. Not to mention all the headaches.

DO YOU DARE TO LIVE AS A MILLIONAIRE?

Those who can find their way in this globalised world can live like a millionaire without being one. You have the tools available to discover your mission (remember the Steve Pavlina exercise), to further develop your mission and to share it with the world (build your Business Model Canvas). And now you also know how you can leave all the tasks you dislike to others who enjoy them more.

So, are you ready to live like a millionaire?

Are you ready to leave The 5% Club and only do what you really love?

Every single day of your life?

CHAPTER 6

LIVING THE DREAM!

SPENDING AS MUCH TIME
AS YOU LIKE ON REALISING
YOUR MISSION, WITH AN
ABUNDANCE OF MONEY.

MY SUNDAY WALK IN THE PARK. THE ASIAN VERSION.

It's early Monday morning. The weather is lovely and sunny, and I feel like spending some time outdoors. You know: observing nature, breathing in the fresh air and simply disconnecting from the everyday rush. But this morning I won't be going to the city park. Nor to the woods or the beach. My outdoor adventure takes place 20 meters below sea level. At 6 o'clock in the morning and with 28 degrees Celsius I jump into the Andaman Sea wearing only my bikini and scuba gear.

My diving buddies are already floating on the water surface. "Come on. The water feels amazing!" I jump off the boat, plunge into the water, feel the warm water surrounding my naked skin, pop up on the surface again and smile. I make the universal diver's sign for 'everything okay'. My dive instructor Steve smiles back at me. "Ready to go and have a look down there?" I nod. And I smile. Let's go! I release the air from my BCD and sink down into the water. Air bubbles everywhere. The only sound is the one of my own breathing. In. Out. In. Out. I am wondering what this morning would have looked like if I were in Belgium. I smile. It doesn't matter. We sink further down. I let my ears pop. We dive a bit deeper. The water is nice and warm and the best shower you can imagine on a Monday morning at 6 am.

My dive instructor Steve is leading our dive. He 'asks' if everything is okay.

Hell yeah!

Twenty meters below sea level and on my right I see Jennifer. She's American, married to Brad, young, pretty and big time fun. A blabbermouth on land but very timid under water. She observes, she swims, she enjoys. I smile and enjoy it too. On my left I see Brad. He is hanging upside down to have a peep in a small hole. According to me, his head is just a bit too close to the hole. But he is having fun, takes pictures and swims from left to right, up and down, on his back, on his side, on his belly and upside down again. I smile and enjoy his underwater circus act. Right in front of me is my instructor Steve. He is my rock. Literally and figuratively. He will rescue me if there is a risk of me drowning. He will supply me with oxygen if I run out of air. He turns around, looks at me and with his thumb and index finger makes the universal under water sign for 'are you okay?' I smile. Of course I am okay. I couldn't have been more okay than this!

WHAT DO YOU DO ON YOUR MOST PERFECT DAY EVER?

If you could design your most perfect day, what would it be like? What would you create? With whom would you spend it? What great cause would you contribute to? Where would you love to be? Which amazing part of you would you want to show to the world?

Visualise it on the next page.

MY PERFECT DAY

LIVING THE DREAM: THE FINAL DESTINATION APPEARS TO BE JUST THE BEGINNING.

The fifth phase. The Ultimate Phase. The phase in which you spend all the time you want on fulfilling your mission whilst enjoying an abundance of money doing it. It is the phase of which everybody who isn't in it yet, thinks that it's only reserved for the lucky millionaires. For years I too believed that this phase was something for the happy few. Until 2011. That is when I read the book 'The 4-Hour Work Week' in which I discovered that you don't have to be a millionaire to live like one. Right now I feel like I live a millionaire's life. Yet I am not one. Living and fulfilling my mission as an Explorer of Life has become a reality and it has been like this for the last couple of years. Discovering my own unique path, escaping from what is considered normal and achievable and radically choosing to do whatever makes my heart sing on a daily basis. Well... that is the best gift I have ever given myself.

I remember very clearly where and when my journey towards a more fulfilling life started: crying on the wooden floor of my apartment, with a screwdriver in my hand. But where will this journey end? I really have no idea. I don't know what the final destination of this dream life will be. And there is no need to know. In fact today I think that there is no ultimate destination... There is no retirement I am waiting for, no next holiday to count down to, no financial goals that need to be reached, no emptiness to be filled.

I have been blessed to discover how to live a life fully in line with my mission. It has been a journey, just like the travels I made during those years. And as with all journeys I also learned that it is not so much about reaching that final destination. It is all about enjoying the waves whilst riding them.

> **❝And if the music is good, you dance!❞**
> **Quote from Happy Feet**

With this book I have offered you an entry ticket to the playground called life. It all starts with discovering what you really love to do in your life and move on from there. Find the courage and the willpower to walk your own unique path, step by step. From one phase to the next. That is how you too can leave your magical footprint on this earth. You can mean an awful lot. Not only to yourself and your family, but to your kids, your friends, the society you live in and the beautiful world which we are co-creating every single day. I have experienced first-hand that when you are fulfilling your mission, you allow your full potential to flourish. You outgrow yourself in a way that you might well have thought of as impossible.

Your dream life is right there, just in front of you. It is up for grabs. If you want it.

No matter what you do and where you are right now in your journey towards a more fulfilled life, there is one thing I can tell you with great certainty. If I were to die tomorrow, I would laugh heartily and shout from the top of my lungs: 'Damn, what a ride!'

EPILOGUE

HOW A SELF-CENTRED ADVENTURE CAN BE OF VALUE TO OTHERS.

Your search for a life filled with passion might feel like a very self-centred adventure. It's all about your mission, your passions, your willpower, your unique path, your company, your dreams etc. This is definitely how it felt to me at times during the last four years.

Was my adventure self-centred? Absolutely!

Would I do it again? Without a doubt!

I consider this adventure and my quest for a more fulfilling life as an ode to myself. It has been a wild celebration of the fantastic life I received when I was born. Today I am in the fifth phase of fulfilling my mission and I feel that I am at a turning point in my life. Once again.

> **"It is not enough to reach the treasure.
> One must bring it back."**
> *Roger Lipsey*

This self-centred adventure of mine lasted almost four years. Four years of mainly focusing on myself. Is that a long time? Is it a short time? I don't know. It was simply the time I needed to pick up the pieces of my old life, look at them and put them back together to form a much more meaningful life. During this period I have often felt fantastic, happy-to-tears and amazed. At times I was also lost, afraid and alone. I started sharing my story during those years. Mainly because people came to me and told me how remarkable it was; the way I had designed my life. They told me that they too would love to live their dreams. But that they couldn't because of X, Y or Z. Although deep down inside me, my adventure felt as an "I really don't know what I am doing and if this is a good idea at all" story, it seemed to be a source of inspiration for all those amazing people I met along the way. And the longer I was stubbornly walking my own unique path, the more people got inspired to do so as well. I'd never expected this to happen, but it just did. And it keeps on happening. I find it magical to be able to inspire others with an adventure that has been so self-centred. Therefore I am very grateful that I can share my story with you through this book.

Love,

Lien

THIS BOOK WOULD NOT EXIST WITHOUT THE HELP OF SO MANY FANTASTIC PEOPLE.

Annelies Baudonck
Without her strong belief in me I would have never wrote the first edition of the Dutch version of this book.

Jana, Kathleen, Dora and some anonymous test readers
They were brave enough to plow through the very first drafts of this book.

Sofie Van Veirdegem
They had the hideous task of translating the initial Dutch version of this book into English.

Everyone who was part of the first Book Launch Team
Without this support team of hundred people I guess my book would have never sold so well and be stored somewhere in a garage getting dust.

Kathleen Steegmans
For her support, her friendship and her illustration work for this book.

Everyone mentioned in this book
For the role they played in my transition from slave to surfer.

Everyone who has been supporting me throughout the years
Friends, family, my professional crew of colleagues, awesome customers I worked with and specifically my mum, who has raised me to the woman I am today.

www.ingramcontent.com/pod-product-compliance
Lightning Source LLC
Chambersburg PA
CBHW051317120626

46547CB00015B/2275